SEX DIFFERENCES:
Social and Biological Perspectives

D1291998

MICHAEL S. TEITELBAUM is Fellow of Nuffield College, Oxford, and University Lecturer in Demography, Oxford University. He received his doctorate in 1970 from Oxford, and has served on the faculty of Princeton University and on the professional staff of the Ford Foundation.

SEX DIFFERENCES:
Social and Biological Perspectives

EDITED AND WITH AN INTRODUCTION BY
MICHAEL S. TEITELBAUM

ANCHOR BOOKS
ANCHOR PRESS/DOUBLEDAY
Garden City, New York

Library of Congress Cataloging in Publication Data

Main entry under title:

Sex differences.

Includes bibliographies and index.
1. Sex differences. 2. Sex role. I. Teitelbaum,
Michael S. [DNLM: 1. Behavior. 2. Sex
characteristics. BF692 S516]
QP251.S482   301.41
ISBN 0-385-00826-0
Library of Congress Catalog Card Number 75–6172

Anchor Books Edition: 1976
Copyright © 1976 by Michael Teitelbaum

CONTENTS

CONTRIBUTORS

Jane Beckman Lancaster, a specialist in primate social behavior and human evolution, was educated at Wellesley College and the University of California at Berkeley. Following completion of her doctorate, she carried out field research in Zambia on the social behavior of the vervet monkey. She has served as a Lecturer at the University of California at Berkeley, as Associate Professor at Rutgers University, and is currently Research Affiliate of the Delta Regional Primate Center in Covington, Louisiana.

Ashton Barfield, a reproductive biologist, did her doctoral work at Princeton University. While still a student, she worked at the Yerkes Primate Center. Later she held a postdoctoral fellowship in the Department of Obstetrics and Gynecology at the University of Pennsylvania Medical School. Currently she is co-ordinating research on male contraceptive methods as a staff member of the International Committee for Contraception Research of the Population Council, New York.

Judith K. Brown, an anthropologist, was educated at Cornell University, Harvard University, and the University of London. She held a postdoctoral fellowship at the Radcliffe Institute, and is currently Assistant Professor of Anthropology at Oakland University, Rochester, Michigan.

Vivien Stewart, a sociologist, received both her undergraduate and graduate education at Oxford University, where she specialized in the sociology of education. Currently she is Program Officer at the Carnegie Corporation of New York, where she is responsible for a program of research, demonstration and litigation grants concerned with educational inequities, including those based upon discrimination by sex.

Elizabeth Fee, a historian of science, was educated at Cambridge University and Princeton University. She has served as Instructor in the History Department of the State University of New York at Binghamton, teaching courses in the history of science and medicine and in women's studies. Currently she is Instructor in Humanities and Archivist at the School of Health Services, Johns Hopkins University.

I. INTRODUCTION

Michael S. Teitelbaum

For most of us, the most salient single descriptive characteristic of a person is his or her sex. Even our language is structured around the sexual dichotomy (he/she, his/her), less so in English, more so in others which ascribe sexual statuses even to inanimate nouns. That sexual categories have great importance in society cannot be sensibly disputed.

In recognition of this fact, most studies of human behavior have recorded and tabulated their results by sex, and the subject of sex differences in behavior has been a legitimate area of study for many years. In recent years the growth of *political* ferment around the social category of sex has been accompanied by a surge of scientific (and pseudoscientific) studies focused specifically upon sex differences, from the sober tomes of academe to the trendy hyperbole of the tabloids.

The effort has not been wasted, for the questions at hand are really quite fundamental ones: *Are* there documentable differences in behavior or abilities between the sexes? If so, can they legitimately be described as *predetermined* tendencies of gene and hormone, or as *manipulable* artifacts of sex-role socialization and the structure of society? Or, finally, is this an inappropriate formulation of a situation which cannot properly be characterized as "either/or"? Since sex is one of the most salient of the dimensions along which most of human society is structured, these questions go to the heart of our interpretation of the social and biological reality in which we live.

In dealing with this fundamental issue of sex

differences, one can make two assertions that are likely
to raise disciplinary hackles among either social or biological scientists:

(1) the human individual is a member of the animal
kingdom, and human behavior is affected mean-
ingfully by biological attributes;

(2) the human individual is an overwhelmingly social animal, and human behavior is influenced
strongly by social forces characteristic of the
species or its subgroups.

Both assertions would appear self-evident to the uninitiated, but one or the other would be rejected or
strongly attacked by some sociologists, anthropologists,
psychologists, ethologists, geneticists, or practitioners of
several other disciplines. The recent vehement debates
over the written and spoken claims of Messrs. Jensen,
Shockley, Herrnstein, and Eysenck illustrate the degree
of scientific acrimony which can be generated over such
ideas. The issue is compounded in dealing with sex
differences in human behavior and ability, for each discipline has defined the term "sex" in a particular way,
with numerous connotations and implied assumptions as
to the source of behavior differences. It is little wonder,
therefore, that in interdisciplinary discussions of sex
differences the participants often talk past one another.

Yet despite such problems, the only sensible approach
to the subject of sex differences is from *both* social and
biological perspectives—for want of a better term we
might call this the "social-biological" approach. This approach is essentially interactive in its theories, data, and
methods. It appears less coherent only because it
presumes to transgress disciplinary boundaries, boundaries which are themselves arbitrarily defined by the intellectual history of the Western world. Many of the
current disciplines which have been formalized in the

Western universities have arisen historically according to the ease with which their subject matter could be studied, and/or chance findings which opened new areas of concern at a particular time. And yet it has become abundantly clear that these arbitrary boundaries, which divide the study of the human species into highly insulated compartments, may well have become counterproductive. There can be little doubt that nascent disciplines often benefit from isolation from other disciplines, allowing them to develop their own body of theory, concepts, data, and methods. At some later point, however, the barriers may serve to sterilize the full-blown discipline from the infection (or fertilization) of outside approaches to similar problems. Indeed, many of the advances in recent years have occurred at the interfaces or boundaries of the traditional disciplines, e.g., biophysics, social psychology, and social medicine.

It is a disturbing fact that the strong barriers of separation between the social and biological sciences are to a substantial degree *political* rather than intellectual. Social scientists often employ analogues of biological concepts, especially in the structure-functional paradigm of social systems and in such terminology as homeostasis, function, structure, etc. Indeed the language of social science since Spencer is soaked in biological terminology. Yet the introduction of explicitly biological *variables,* as opposed to concepts and terminology, into social science discussions often leads to a *political* reaction on the part of social scientists. The source of this reaction is no mystery at all. Historically, it has its origin in the period surrounding the turn of the twentieth century, when the simplistic application of biological knowledge to the interpretation of social relations was used as a "scientific" legitimation of reactionary political ideologies. The intellectual history of this debate

is therefore of importance in understanding the current
status of social-biological approaches to the study of the
human species in general, and of human sex differences
in particular. The remainder of this Introduction consists of a brief description of the scientific and political
bases of this historical (and historic) debate about the
general relationships among social and biological forces
in human behavior. The social-biological nature of sex
differences is then assessed in the five chapters which
follow.

A Brief History of Social-biological Thought

Malthusian Origins: One of the intellectual progenitors
of nineteenth-century social-biological thought was the
Reverend Thomas Malthus, a Cambridge-educated
minister of the Church of England, whose lifetime,
from 1766 to 1834, spanned the period of the French
and American revolutions. Malthus' basic argument
was that mankind's biological ability to reproduce itself
outweighed its ability to produce the necessities of life,
particularly food. In his first *Essay on the Principle of
Population* in 1798, he asserted that populations increase
in geometric progressions (i.e., 1, 2, 4, 16, 32, 64,
. . .), while subsistence increases arithmetically (i.e.,
1, 2, 3, 4, 5, 6, 7, 8, . . .). On the basis of these assertions his argument distilled to the now well-known
truism that geometrically increasing growth must easily
outstrip arithmetically increasing growth. (Such a position has recently been brought up to date in a techno-
logical sense by the highly promoted computer projec-
tions of the Club of Rome Report entitled *The Limits
to Growth* [7]).

Writing in 1798, Malthus assumed an innate capacity
of human populations living under favorable environmental circumstances to double every twenty-five years.

(Actually this was probably a good estimate of the situation in the United States at that time.) With such a brief doubling time, it was evident to Malthus that population growth rates would have to be checked. He described two types of checks:

(1) *Positive checks,* which increased the *death* rate via "misery" and "vice." Here Malthus described the effects of famine, war, and disease.

(2) *Preventive checks,* which reduced the *birth* rate. Here Malthus spoke of "moral restraint," by which he meant postponement of marriage, non-marriage, and celibacy outside marriage.

One of Malthus' important propositions was that too rapid a population growth was the fundamental cause of poverty. This assertion undoubtedly reflected a political bias on his part. Indeed, one of his major reasons for writing the essay in the first place was to counteract the utopian socialism of Godwin and Condorcet. The essay was then in part a political tract, and was treated as such by later commentators on the subject.

The importance of Malthus has little to do with his correctness. As a predictor of the future growth of population and food supply, Malthus was wrong. From the period of his essay to the present, food supply has on average grown faster than population. As a prescription of what ought to be done, Malthus' views were not followed. For Malthus never made a clear reference to the practice of contraception, which now has become almost universal in the developed countries. He may have considered it to be "vice," or he may have viewed it as merely ineffectual. Eventually, however, he did come to the position that preventive checks such as "moral restraint" might be more effective than he had initially supposed.

The significance of Malthus, then, is that he presented the first well-known treatment of population as a social-biological issue. Malthus' argument affected Darwin's biological thought and also the sociological writings of Herbert Spencer and the economic theories of Ricardo. Finally, Malthus' essay stimulated the attention (and the criticism) of Karl Marx. In his writings on the intrinsically social-biological issue of population growth and its relationship to food supply, Malthus most certainly did not provide the appropriate answers. He did, however, open the issue to widespread discussion, and stimulated serious and intensive debate among the leading intellectual figures of the nineteenth century.

Darwinian Biology: The Malthusian hypothesis had the greatest impact upon Charles Robert Darwin. Darwin, like Malthus, had studied theology and medicine. In 1831, he was offered the post (unpaid) of Naturalist aboard HMS *Beagle* on a journey to South America to collect geographical information. The five-year journey gave him the raw material for his later insights into evolution,* although it was not until twenty-three years later that he wrote his seminal book *On the Origin of Species*. Yet we know that as early as 1837 Darwin knew at least the following (5):

(1) Species vary over space. He knew this from his own extensive observations during the HMS *Beagle* expedition.

---

* It also cost him his health. Darwin probably suffered until he died from a disease known as Chagas disease. This disease was not identified until 1909, and is the result of a parasitic infection of the heart and intestines by a bacterium called *Trypanosoma cruzi*, carried by the insect known colloquially as Benchuca (*Triatoma infestans*). Darwin describes this insect in great detail, and wrote of one of them biting his finger and sucking blood while he was in Peru (5).

(2) Species succeed one another over time. This he knew from the work of Sedgwick and Lyell on geology.

(3) Random and heritable traits accumulate as a result of artificial selection practices. This he knew from the extensive experience of breeders of dogs and livestock.

However, he was unable to understand how these facts related to *natural* selection until he happened upon Malthus' *Essay on the Principle of Population* in 1838. He describes the effect of this essay on his thought: "It at once struck me that under these circumstances [of struggle for existence], favourable variations would tend to be preserved, and unfavourable ones to be destroyed. The result of this would be the formation of a new species. Here, then, I had at last got a theory by which to work (3)." Darwin wrote out a draft of his theory in 1844 but waited twelve years to begin writing intensively. Then, in 1858, he was shocked when he received from Alfred Wallace a manuscript on evolution with a theory almost identical to his own. This prompted him to publish his theory in November of 1859, after previously publishing a brief summary of his views jointly with Wallace's manuscript (5).

The original title of Darwin's *magnum opus* was *On the Origin of Species by Means of Natural Selection, or the Preservation of Favoured Races in the Struggle for Life*. Later, on Wallace's suggestion, he changed the title to Herbert Spencer's formulation: the phrase "Survival of the Fittest" replaced "Preservation of Favoured Races." Unfortunately, this change of wording led to semantic obfuscation of his major point. For the essential feature of Darwin's theory of natural selection is not mere survival; it is the *differential reproductivity* of individuals who are favored adaptively by

chance variation which leads to an increasing proportion of similarly constituted offspring in a population.

The basic arguments of Darwinian theory are as follows:

(1) New species appear.
(2) New species have evolved from old species.
(3) Evolution of species is the result of natural selection.
(4) Natural selection depends on variation, which
continues despite the tendency of natural selection to eliminate "unfit" variants.

The critical Darwinian contribution were items 3 and 4.
Natural selection is the struggle among individuals in
the context of environmentally limited resources. An organism which is able to survive and to outreproduce
others is an evolutionally "superior" organism, according to Darwinian theory. The key point here is that it is
reproduction, not simply survival, that is the engine of
natural selection. By reproducing, the superior organism
will pass on to the next generation the superior traits
which it possessed. The inferior traits are not reproduced to the same degree and eventually die out over a
long time span. The struggle to survive and to reproduce is based upon variations among individuals. For
Darwin, the source of these variations was *not genetic
but primarily environmental;* that is, he believed in the
inheritance of acquired traits. Indeed, Darwin did not
know of the genetic research of Gregor Mendel, whose
work was published obscurely in 1865, and which did
not become widely known until after the turn of the
twentieth century.

Social Darwinian Thought: The remarkable theoretical
advances of Darwinian theory had great intellectual impact on late-nineteenth-century thinkers, and the fer-

ment was by no means restricted to evolutionary biology. Social thinkers, too, sought insight into the origin and the nature of human society through the application of Darwinian analysis. Hence the metamorphosis of Darwinian biological theory into "Social Darwinian" social theory was an understandable, if scientifically unsupportable, progression. The key propositions which developed as the core of Social Darwinian theory may be simplified as follows:

Proposition 1: The less fit varieties will be eliminated or subordinated, and the more fit will survive and dominate.

Proposition 2: Inequalities are natural among individuals, and are maintained via the "invariant" process of inheritance.

Proposition 3: Natural inequalities include ability and morality, leading to unequal ownership of property (also "natural") and therefore a "natural" stratification system.

Proposition 4: Since inheritance of inequality is an invariant process, it follows that the perpetuation of the current "natural" system of stratification is also "natural."

COROLLARY: Any attempt to mitigate existing or future inequalities (via welfare legislation, socialism, redistributive taxes, etc.) is contrary to nature and will either fail or will lead to a diminution of the quality of society.

Here, then, was an apparently powerful scientific justification for the conservative ideology of laissez-faire. The leading intellectual contribution of the century was proof for all to see of the validity and conformity with nature of the economic and social status quo. Conservative ideology had been combined with Darwinian concepts to produce a "social-biological" theory of society which justified the existing class and economic structure of late-nineteenth-century society. Such political uses of biological concepts, as we shall see, became a major source of the schism between the social and biological sciences.

Social Darwinian theory was widely disseminated in England and the United States by a number of prominent social and biological scientists. The first and perhaps the most influential was Herbert Spencer, the great contributor to the theory of social order, a strong exponent of individualism in society, and the man who coined the unfortunate phrase "survival of the fittest," used by Darwin. Others included Walter Bagehot and William Graham Sumner. Social Darwinism became a powerful intellectual force and engendered social movements which sought to fend off as biologically deleterious any attempts on the part of government to intervene in the "selective" process of the laissez-faire system.

Eugenics: There was another movement with a social-biological perspective which derived from rather similar origins, combining a concern with the genetic effects of social policy with a conservative political ideology. This movement, known as Eugenics, was founded by Sir Francis Galton at the end of the nineteenth century. Since this occurred before the rediscovery of Mendel's laws of inheritance, its original scientific foundations were shaky. And it too, like Social Darwinism, soon became wedded to the class and economic ideologies of many of its prominent proponents.

The basic tenet of Eugenics was that human progress may be furthered by genetic as well as cultural means. It noted that the human species had evolved a superior neural capacity through genetic processes, and that the only known genetic means for such progress was natural or artificial selection of heritable traits. The Eugenicists held, however, that natural selection in its modern form had become deleterious to the quality of the human species. They noted with dismay a tendency for families of lower socioeconomic groups (who according to their definitions also had lower levels of innate intelligence) to have large numbers of children, while professional and upper-class families had few children. This led them to express great concern that the average intelligence of the population must be declining. At the same time they attributed the increasing incidences of crime, insanity, poverty, and mental deficiency which they perceived to the differentially high reproductive rates of the groups of people characterized by these social "flaws." As with the case of intelligence, they saw these traits as genetically heritable.

Given their perception of the deleterious effects of natural-selective processes, the Eugenicists advocated the use of *artificial* selection as a means of increasing the relative contribution to the following generation of the "superior" individuals. Here the Eugenicists diverged from the laissez-faire ideology of the Social Darwinists, for their approach was strongly interventionist. They sought to encourage the reproduction of those who had genetically determined characteristics defined as "good" and to restrict the reproduction of those with characteristics defined as "bad." Various incentives to increase reproduction were suggested, including financial incentives and educational campaigns concerning the risk of the differential rates of reproduction. Alexander Graham Bell, who in addition to his inventive activities was one of the supporters of the Eugenics movement, stated that "The individuals have power to improve the race but not the knowledge of what to do. We students of genetics possess the knowledge but not the power; and the great hope lies in the dissemination of our knowledge among the people at large (2)." And in 1910, former President Theodore Roosevelt wrote, "Some day we will realize that the prime duty, the inescapable duty, of the *good* citizen of the right type is to leave his or her blood behind him in the world; and that we have no business to permit the perpetuation of citizens of the wrong type (9)."

The positive incentives to greater reproduction of the "good" elements in society was never a feasible political program, however, and the Eugenicists slowly moved to the negative incentives hinted at in the last part of Roosevelt's statement: the restriction of reproduction among the "bad" elements of society. There were two major groups following this approach. The first, guided primarily by psychiatrists, psychologists, and social reformers interested in the prevention of disease, crime, and mental deficiency, pursued their goals through intensive campaigns for restriction of marriage, custodial care, and/or sterilization for the "unfit." This campaign was remarkably effective in the United States. By the 1930s, fully forty-one states had passed marriage limitation laws, and thirty had passed sterilization laws for the mentally defective. In addition to these statutes, laws were passed in support of compulsory commitment of mental defectives to mental institutions, which effectively precluded reproduction for the large majority of those committed without the necessity of sterilization. Many of these laws remain in the law books to this day, but most were never enforced effectively (6:124–143).

The second thread of the Eugenics movement in the United States was represented by those who saw genetic deterioration in the large-scale immigration to the United States of persons from eastern and southern Europe. Most of the supporters of this position were members of families deriving from the earlier flow of immigration to America from western and northern Europe, and who feared that the new "races" of immigrants were biologically inferior to the older "races" and would be unable to adapt to American culture and democratic principles. This concern found a strong basis in the quasi-scientific theories of Eugenics, which gradually had been moving from a concern over the genetic constitution of *individuals* to a derived concern over the genetic constitution of entire *populations* such as "races." This part of the Eugenics movement too was politically potent and legislatively effective. With the support of the leadership of the American Federation of Labor, who were disturbed by the impact of heavy immigration flows upon wages and working conditions, the Eugenics movement directed its first campaign at the enactment of a literacy test to be applied to potential immigrants. Such a test was adopted by Congress in 1913 but vetoed by President Taft. It was again passed in 1915 but vetoed by President Wilson. Finally in 1917 the bill was enacted over President Wilson's veto. This law also established an Asiatic Zone from which all immigration was excluded. The satisfaction of the Eugenicists with this notable legislative success turned to ashes, however, when they realized that only a few immigrants from the "less desirable" areas of the world failed to pass the literacy test. The law became then only the first in an inexorable legislative progression toward eugenic restriction of immigration. The final fruition of this movement was the immigration law adopted as permanent policy by Congress in 1924, in which racial considerations were foremost. The law restricted immigration from each nation to 2 per cent of the foreign-born from that country according to the U.S. census of 1890, and also effectively excluded all Orientals. The census in 1890 was chosen over the census of

1910 because the proportion of Americans of northern and western European origin was considerably higher in the earlier census (6:144–59).

Sociological Response: While the intellectual movement and political forces underlying Social Darwinism and Eugenics were developing, there was also a strain of thought which ran utterly counter to their tendencies. The eventual leader of this movement was a distinguished botanist and paleo-botanist, Lester Ward. In 1883 Ward published his *magnum opus, Dynamic Sociology* (12) while he was the chief paleontologist in the U. S. Geological Survey. Later he became Professor of Sociology at Brown University.

Ward's *Dynamic Sociology* appeared at the early stages of the development of sociology. Indeed, at this time William Graham Sumner was perhaps the only academic using the term "sociology." Ward's work had profound effect on the development of the nascent discipline. He was the first president of the American Sociological Society, and two of the later leaders of the discipline, Albion W. Small and Edward A. Ross, attributed many of their ideas to Ward. Yet Ward, unlike Sumner, never enjoyed general public acclaim.

Ward's origins were lower-class, and he was deeply affronted by the elitist tendencies of Social Darwinism. His politics and his science told him that the ideology of Social Darwinism was poor politics and poor science. He argued that the application of natural law to social theory ignored the clear fact that nature itself is grossly uneconomic. Reproductive wastage of most organisms was enormous, and by analogy, industrial competition was itself similarly wasteful. He held that human will distinguished human processes from the blind natural forces of genetics. Man had shown that he had great superiority over his environment, and to Ward the continuing enthusiasm of the theorists of laissez-faire for natural law was merely a primitive religion. Man should not be controlled by the laws of nature but rather should study them and direct them. The principle of survival of the fittest in the struggle for existence was the economics of animals, who could not control their numbers within the available resources. In contrast the human species plans ahead, carries on agriculture, digs wells, and controls its numbers, thus distinguishing human economics from that of animals. Hence, "while environment transforms the animal, man transforms the environment (7:74)."

In short, while Ward agreed that the origins of man were determined by natural selection and that his superior intellect was the product of that evolutionary process, he also believed that with these intellectual resources man could become superior to other animals by supplanting genetic progress with progress determined by the application of intelligence to man's problems. Indeed, it appears that Ward continued to believe some of the Lamarckian notions of the transmission of acquired characteristics.

Ward did not seek to disguise his aim of destroying the tradition of biological sociology. He had a running battle with what he perceived as the overly optimistic views of the Spencerians and the equally overly pessimistic views of the Malthusians. He applied a form of class analysis to these approaches, viewing them as upper-class apologies for reactionary politics (7). He viewed Malthusian theory in particular as a fundamental law of biology but felt that in applying it to *Homo sapiens* Malthus had chosen the one species for which it was not appropriate.

Notwithstanding the failure of Malthusianism at all points, the impression prevailed, and still prevails, that it is a fundamental law of society, and the current sociology is based upon it . . . The fact is that man and society are not, except in a very limited sense, under the influence of the great dynamic laws that control the rest of the animal world . . . If we call biologic processes natural, we must call social processes artificial. The fundamental principle of biology is natural selection, that of sociology is artificial selection. The survival of the fittest is simply the survival of the strong, which implies and would better be called the destruction of the weak. If nature progresses through the destruction of the weak, man progresses through the protection of the weak (14).

Ward (like most other professional biologists of his period) was unconvinced by facile analogies between nature and society. He was also disturbed by the political motivation of those so committed to these analogies, though his attacks upon them were based in part upon his own political beliefs. Because of his impact upon the development of American sociology, his point of view on biological sociology was an important factor in the intellectual history of the discipline. In addition, his disciple Small made special efforts to promote his critical views among sociologists. Sociology consciously separated itself from biology, and the tendency arose to base sociological studies on psychological rather than biological concepts. Small summarized the new view of the earlier biologistic sociology of Spencer thus:

Mr. Herbert Spencer has been a much mixed blessing . . . He has probably done more than any man of recent times to set a fashion of semi-learned thought, but he has lived to hear himself pronounced an anachronism by men who were once his disciples . . . Spencer's principles of sociology are supposed principles of biology extended to cover social relations. But the decisive factors in social relations are understood by present sociologists to be psychical, not biological (10).

As the discipline developed, such attitudes became dominant. Even supporters of the biologistic approach, such as Giddings, conceded that "the attempt to construct a science of society by means of biological analogies had been abandoned by all serious investigators of social phenomena (4)." As early as 1909 Baldwin commented that "the attempt . . . very current at one time . . . to interpret social organization by strict analogy with the physical organism is now discredited. Such a view will not stand before the consideration of the most elementary psychological principles (1)."

Hence there arose in sociological thought a strict aversion to biological analogies and even to biological concepts. In reaction to the excesses of the Social Darwinists and Eugenicists, sociologists took to defining social behavior as wholly defined by psychological and social factors. The pendulum swung to the other extreme—from facile arguments by analogy to facile dismissal of theory and evidence. Thus the views of many sociologists toward biological data and concepts took on an ideological cast in two senses: first, in the sense of a disciplinary ideology opposing the reductionist incursions of another previously "imperialistic" discipline†; and second, in the political ideology of opposition to the social views of those urging biological sociology—the Social Darwinists and Eugenicists. Emotional revulsion from the atrocities committed by the Nazis in the name of biological "truths" reinforced their rejection of the biologistic view of human society.

Such tendencies continue in modern sociology in

---

† Of course, there were also legitimate arguments against improper reductionism in science. See, for example, Ernest Nagel, *The Structure of Science* (New York: Harcourt, Brace & World, 1961), pp. 336–97.

more muted form. Professional sociological literature rarely sees mention of biological factors as contributing in any way to social behavior. Some leading theorists of modern sociology dismiss biological factors as of minor importance, and there is a generalized suspicion of those who argue that biological factors do have some impact upon human social behavior. Such a perception is strongly reinforced by the recent reincarnation of biological-determinism theories, including those on racial differences in intelligence and those on sex differences in behavior and abilities. The excessive claims by advocates of these theories have provoked the same type of response among modern sociologists as was provoked in their intellectual forebears by the Social Darwinists and Eugenicists.

Sex as a Social-biological Characteristic

The scientific literature, both historical and modern, is replete with materials arguing that one or another sexual characteristic is *either* social *or* biological in its origins. Yet in the absence of disciplinary blinders, it is clear that sex is *both* a social *and* a biological characteristic. The primary objective of this book is to examine human sex differences from this social-biological perspective.

In Chapter II immediately following, Jane Lancaster presents a careful and concise evaluation of the findings and implications of sex-role behavior in the higher primates. She shows that much of what was thought to be revealed wisdom and was popularized by Tiger (12) and others is in fact based upon incomplete and apparently incorrect data. Dr. Lancaster outlines the current state of knowledge in this important area, and highlights the pitfalls lying before those willing to make facile extrapolations from animal behavior to human behavior, especially when understanding of the former is only partial and tentative.

There has been a wealth of research on the nature and extent of direct biological influences upon behavioral differences between the sexes. In Chapter III, Ashton Barfield presents a comprehensive survey and evaluation of this material. She shows that such biological influences do exist, but that the sociocultural system also has major impact. A simple-minded denial of physical, medical, and psychological differences between the sexes cannot be supported by the evidence; but neither can the attribution of all such differences to genetic and biological factors.

The sources of the well-documented division of labor by sex in virtually all societies is discussed by Judith Brown in Chapter IV. While there is considerable literature which hypothesizes that this dimension of societal differentiation is structured along lines of physical, biological, and psychological differences between the sexes, the empirical evidence shows that this hypothetical position is quite insufficient. Once again the biologically based sex differences are a component, but are not "the" determinant of observed differences in behavior between the sexes.

In Chapter V, Vivien Stewart brings the sociological and psychological literature on sex-role socialization to bear upon the full complexity of interrelationships among personality, ability, and achievement. She also deals with such issues as the effect of the mother upon the sex-role development of the child as compared with that of the father, and with the implications of this for the increasingly common phenomenon of the single-parent family. Her chapter thus provides a cogent evaluation of current knowledge regarding the relative contributions of family, school, media, and peers to the process of sex-role development, and point to the gaps and ambiguities which remain to be solved.

Finally, in Chapter VI, Elizabeth Fee places the discussion of sex differences in historical perspective. Her illuminating discussion shows how the social and ideological forces at work in the rapidly industrializing societies of Great Britain and the United States in the sixty years from 1860 to 1920 had major impact upon the focus, and indeed, even the findings, of scientific research endeavor. Her analysis is an appropriate final chapter, for it illustrates well the political components of earlier "scientific" discussions of sex differences which may now appear merely amusing. The long history of political ideology in discussions of social-biological factors such as sex differences suggests the importance of examining modern scientific assumptions and methodologies, thereby seeking to avoid a 1970s reincarnation of the pseudoscience of only two generations ago. This book is offered as a modest contribution toward that end.

References

1. Baldwin, James Mark, 1909. *Darwin and the Humanities.* Baltimore: Review Publishing Co., p. 40. (Cited in 7:158)
2. Bell, Alexander Graham, 1914. "How to Improve the Race." *Journal of Heredity,* V, 1. (Cited in 6:81)
3. Darwin, Charles Robert, 1887. *Autobiography of Charles Darwin, 1809–1882.* (Nora Barlow, ed.) London: Collins, p. 120 (1958 edition).
4. Giddings, Franklin H., 1900. *Democracy and Empire.* New York: The Macmillan Co., p. 29. (Cited in 7:158).
5. Gillespie, Charles C., 1968. "Charles Darwin." Pp. 7–14 in *International Encyclopedia of the Social Sciences,* Volume 4. New York: Crowell Collier and Macmillan.

6. Haller, Mark H., 1963. *Eugenics: Hereditarian Attitudes in American Thought*. New Brunswick: Rutgers University Press.

7. Hofstadter, Richard, 1955. *Social Darwinism in American Thought* (revised edition). Boston: Beacon Press.

8. Meadows, Donnella H., and others, 1972. *The Limits to Growth: a report for the Club of Rome's project on the predicament of mankind*. New York: Universe Books.

9. Roosevelt, Theodore. Personal correspondence cited in 6:81.

10. Small, Albion, 1897. "The Principles of Sociology." *American Journal of Sociology*, II, 741–42. (Cited in 7:159).

11. Sumner, William Graham, 1883. *What social classes owe to each other*. New York: Harper & Bros., pp. 144–45.

12. Tiger, Lionel, 1969. *Men in groups*. New York: Random House.

13. Ward, Lester, 1883. *Dynamic sociology*. New York: Appleton and Co. (2 volumes).

14. Ward, Lester, 1893. *The psychic factors of civilization*. Boston: Ginn and Co., pp. 134–35. (Cited in 7:79)

II. SEX ROLES IN PRIMATE SOCIETIES

JANE BECKMAN LANCASTER

Introduction

Because of the almost "overnight" discovery of both
effective birth control and the reality of the population
explosion, many modern societies have come to the
point where they can realistically ask whether it is necessary or even advisable for all women to become
mothers or for any woman to become a mother more
than once or twice. In less than ten years this question
has changed from an idle, esoteric musing to a vital
concern of most modern societies and soon perhaps of
the whole world. For the first time in human history
there is a need to know what differences in behavior between men and women really exist and whether these
differences are in some way biologically fixed or are
heavily influenced by experience and the social environment. Societies which decide to limit the growth of their
populations and keep family size down to one or two
children will seek new roles for women to play. Certainly few modern societies can afford to keep women
in the relatively unproductive role of housekeeper for
thirty or forty post-family years simply because they
were mothers of small children in their twenties and
early thirties. New roles for women pose numerous
problems and questions for which science and history
offer very few answers. The relationship between biology and experience in determining differences in behavior between the sexes is so infinitely complex that, at
this stage of research, each new piece of data simply
raises more questions than it answers. One of the first

places to look for answers is in the primate heritage of our species, because there we can find patterns which form similarities and continuities with human behavior, and we can also find sharp contrasts which will highlight specializations peculiar to human beings.

During the past fifteen years many biologists and social scientists have tried to develop a balanced view of the reality of human nature—a view which appreciates the evolutionary biology of the species as well as its highly evolved capacity to learn. There have been numerous attempts to synthesize the results of laboratory and field studies on primates and to use these studies to develop an evolutionary framework to study man and human evolution (2, 7, 27, 41, 42). Some of these, such as the books of Ardrey, Tiger, and Morris have been highly popularized best-sellers. Unfortunately most of them suffer from premature generalizations based on the first "round" of ethologically oriented field and laboratory studies, especially in respect to understanding both sex roles and the major features of social organization. Many of the early primate studies had assumed that the behavior patterns they described were species-specific adaptations and that these defined patterns were unlikely to vary significantly within a given species. In fact, some authors even tried to extrapolate from the social organization of a single group of monkeys to the analysis of the social behavior of other primates, including humans. In less than a decade this situation was self-correcting simply because more fully developed studies were done on a larger variety of primate species in a variety of habitats.

It is now quite clear that, contrary to the original assumption, the social structure and social behavior of many primate species are strongly influenced by habitat (9). For example, the original field studies on savannah baboons by DeVore, Hall, and the Altmanns (1, 8,

11), have been supplemented by studies of baboons living in forested areas (29, 30, 31, 34). The social organization of the forest baboon is now known to be much more open and less dominance oriented than is that of the savannah baboon. Even such classic baboon behavior patterns as male sexual jealousy and competition for estrous females is lacking in some of the forest groups. It appears that many of the more terrestrial primates (baboons, macaques, langurs, and vervet monkeys) have quite wide ranges of potential behavior in their repertoires and that group traditions and ecological setting heavily influence, but do not determine, how these patterns will be expressed. This change in perspective has not yet been fully appreciated by some synthesizers. Therefore, many general books on the subject are out of date before they are published. This problem too will be self-correcting with time, as new syntheses and theories are developed based on a wider background of knowledge about primate social behavior.

The Mother-infant Bond and the Matrifocal Subunit

It is an unfortunate and now-recognized fact that many of the early field studies of monkeys and apes suffered from an overemphasis on the behavior of adult males. Adult male primates are often large and their behavior conspicuous. Even though they constitute only a small percentage of the total membership of a primate society, usually somewhere between 10 and 20 per cent, they often get more than their share of an observer's attention unless careful sampling techniques are used. From this bias in observations, it has been only a very short step to see the social relations between that small minority of adult males as equivalent to the social organization of the group.

Another source of bias in the early field studies of

primates came from the length of the study itself. Early workers considered a full study should include the entire year so that seasonal variations in social behavior would not be missed. No one thought that a full year might not be enough to reveal the major outline of social organization in a monkey or ape group. Schaller's classic study (37) on the mountain gorilla was a monumental scientific achievement and yet it involved only nine months of study on a single population and 458 actual hours of observation under very difficult conditions. Today some field workers even discount statistical data from the first hundred or more hours of observation because of the time it takes to get familiar with all the members of the society and the major patterns of interaction.

By the middle of the 1960s, after the first round of primate studies had been published, it seemed to some that the major axis of social organization in primate groups was dominance. Repeatedly, studies on very different species of monkeys and apes reported on the dominance relations of the group. Most often some sort of linear hierarchy was reported, with adult males usually ranking at the top, and females and young below them. Then new material began to flow from three separate ongoing studies: Van Lawick-Goodall's study of chimpanzees begun in Tanzania in 1960, numerous studies on the Japanese macaque begun in the 1950s by members of the Japanese Monkey Center, and long-term behavioral observation begun in 1956 on a free-ranging rhesus macaque colony on Cayo Santiago, an island off Puerto Rico. These three study areas yielded a wealth of material on another major axis of social organization in monkey and ape societies: the mother-infant bond which ramifies through time into a "mother-focused" or matrifocal subunit. The one thing that all these studies have in common is that they are all long-term endeavors, some of which begin to approximate the actual life expectancy of an individual.

Sade (35) demonstrated that the closeness between mother and infant does not end with weaning or even with the assumption of adulthood. He observed a group of rhesus monkeys living on the island colony off Puerto Rico. Among rhesus monkeys grooming is a major form of social interaction. During periods of rest and relaxation a group of rhesus will break up into clusters of social groomers. Grooming is clearly a very pleasurable activity among many primates. It is a self-rewarding behavior pattern in that monkeys who groom seem to be as involved and to enjoy themselves just as much as the individuals who are being groomed. Grooming is undoubtedly one of the major ways in which social bonds are expressed and maintained. Sade became interested in what social factors influenced the choice of grooming partners. He found that the colony was ideal for this because genealogical records had been kept for a number of years preceding his study. On the basis of these records, he established that the overwhelming factor in choosing a grooming partner was that of a close emotional bond based on the mother-young tie. Even during the excitement of the mating season when grooming between mating pairs usually precedes and follows copulation, the frequency of grooming between close relatives was unaltered. For example, one fully mature male was observed to direct 40 per cent of his grooming activities to his mother with no change when he consorted with estrous females. However, she directed only 9 per cent of her grooming toward him because he was only the eldest of her three sons. Sade noted that a mother usually received a larger share of her offspring's grooming than the offspring received of hers—her orientation was to her entire family with special attention for the youngest. Presumably as the years passed and more infants were born, the mother had less and less time for each individual (some females had as many as six or seven offspring living with them), but her older offspring learned that they could easily find partners among their siblings for grooming, resting, and feeding, even if the mother was too busy. In this way the original bond between mother and infant was never really broken because of the need for attention of each new sibling. Instead the original one-to-one bond ramified to include subsequent offspring and even generations among those animals which an individual monkey could count on for affection, comfort, and support.

The ramification of the mother-infant bond to include many individuals belonging to two or more generations forms a special kind of subgroup common to many primate societies. This subgroup is called a "matrifocal" unit because ultimately the bonds that attract these individuals to each other are based on their commonly held focus of attention and emotion, a mother or even a grandmother. There is no such thing as a "patrifocal," or a father-focused unit in monkey and ape societies because for the most part mating systems are promiscuous and the social role of "father" does not exist. Special relations do exist between young animals and particular adult males, but these males are most likely to be an older brother or even a mother's brother, rather than a male with whom mother frequently mates.

The matrifocal unit probably exists in all primate societies, but there is a wide range of variability in how important it is in the daily lives of individuals. There may be a tendency for matrifocal units to become very significant in groups where the survival rate of young animals is relatively high and where group size is big. When the matrifocal group is relatively large, at any one time there are always suitable partners for groom-

ing, resting or feeding and the individual does not have
to look outside the family for a social partner. However, there are also species differences in the ex-
clusiveness of the mother-infant bond and the resulting matrifocal subgroup. Kaufman (16) has reported
on a fascinating series of laboratory observations of two
species of macaque: the bonnet macaque from South
India and the pigtail macaque from Southeast Asia. Although closely related, these two species seem to have
major differences in social responses which greatly
affect the social organization of the group. First of all,
bonnet macaques like to be physically close whenever
possible, so when resting or sleeping, they cluster into a
huddle. Pigtail macaques, which are just as social as the
bonnets, prefer to maintain some distance between each
other, the only exception being a mother with her infant
whom she jealously protects from contacts with other
group members. Bonnet macaques are oriented toward
the entire social group for body contact, comfort, and
the expression of affection. Mothers, of course, play
special roles to their infants, but other females and even
males will show maternal and protective responses.
When Kaufman and his coworker Rosenblum removed
a bonnet mother from her group, her infant was cared
for and protected by other group members. Sometimes
the bonnet infant was virtually adopted by another female, and when his mother was returned to the group
he did not go to her. In contrast pigtail macaques have
a very exclusive relationship between mother and infant, and separation was very traumatic for both. The
infant first showed agitated distress and then depression.
When it tried to get comfort from other females, they
generally ignored it and sometimes even harassed it.
When the mother was returned, there was a dramatic
reunion as mother and offspring rushed into each other's
arms.

Kaufman and Rosenblum found that by the time the colonies were ten years old, there was a dramatic contrast between the two species in social organization. Bonnet macaques showed generalized or diffuse orientation toward the entire social group for grooming, resting, and sleeping partners, whereas the pigtails showed a strong development of three generational, matrifocal subunits including a mother, her offspring (both male and female), and the offspring of her daughters.

Unfortunately, pigtail macaques live in swampy areas with thick vegetation, and long-term studies on them in the wild have proven to be very difficult. Presumably, there is an adaptive advantage for pigtail macaques or the rhesus macaques (studied by Sade) for life in social groups which have two levels of orientation, one to the group as a whole and the other to the matrifocal subunit. In contrast, bonnet macaques and some other types of monkey, like the more arboreal langurs, live in groups where the mother-infant bond is de-emphasized and individuals tend to be oriented toward the entire group. In langurs this diffuse orientation begins at birth when the newborn is passed around from female to female to be held and inspected. Undoubtedly both heredity and experience play important roles in the development of these differences. A pigtail infant, raised from birth by a relaxed, permissive bonnet mother might have very different feelings about his mother and the social group than if he had been raised by his possessive, true mother. That he would act exactly like a bonnet macaque is unlikely, but it would also be highly unlikely that he would grow up to be a typical pigtail macaque either.

In situations where the survival rate of young animals is high and the focus on the mother-infant bond strong, genealogies can become very large and include a number of generations. For example, the Arashiyama

troop of Japanese macaques has been under observation
since 1953 (20). In 1966 this group contained sixteen
genealogies with a total of 163 living members and another 23 known members which had either left the
troop or died. The top ranks of the group were held by
3 old sisters and their brother, and taken all together
they and their living descendants totaled 39 individuals.
There were numerous cases of three generations living
together as well as a few examples of four generations.
Here membership in a genealogy determined most of
the daily decisions that an individual was likely to
make; for example grooming, resting, sleeping, feeding,
play, and traveling companions were most likely to
come from within the genealogy, particularly if it was a
high-ranking one. It was even much easier for a monkey of any age to learn new behavior patterns from a
member of its own genealogy than from unrelated
group members.

The Matrifocal Core

Both field and captive-colony studies suggest that it is
the matrifocal core which provides a primate group
with stability and continuity through time. A field
worker, returning after an absence of a few years, may
only recognize his group through the adult females.
Most of the males he knew may have dispersed among
neighboring groups during his absence. Many different
studies on both terrestrial and arboreal monkeys and
apes indicate that it is the male of the species that is
most likely to wander (3, 10, 13, 23, 32). Males begin
to wander at puberty. They are not necessarily os-
tracized, peripheralized members of low status, or sub-
jugated subadults, but rather they are adventurers. Females, too, change groups on occasion but at a very low
rate compared to males. Koford (18) found that over a

four-year period at Cayo Santiago there were 151
changes between groups, 91 per cent by males. There
are a few scattered reports from studies in the wild of
female monkeys and apes changing groups (32, 37,
22). In these instances the females were young adults,
some with infants. The Japanese data suggest that when
an adult female changes groups it can be a much more
serious affair than when a male does. The female is
likely to take her entire genealogy with her and she may
in effect not change groups so much as she will establish
a new one (20). Among wild groups the rate of male
changes is unclear, but in at least three terrestrial monkeys (vervets, rhesus macaques, and baboons) it is
known to be very high and it is probably even higher in
arboreal groups. For example, Gartlan (10) found that
only one male out of a total of six stayed with his
main study group of vervet monkeys for the entire thir-
teen-month period of observation. Gartlan felt this was
particularly significant because vervet monkeys defend
their group's territory against inroads from neighboring
groups. One would expect that if anything would reduce
male wandering, it would be territorial defense. On
many occasions he saw males change between neighboring groups and within days vigorously defend their new
territories against their former comrades.

There are significant implications from this contrast
between males and females in their rates of mobility between groups. Monkey and ape societies are attached to
specific home ranges or territories even though individuals may not be. Terrestrial and semiterrestrial species
tend to have large home ranges and to eat a wide variety of scattered and seasonal foods. This means that
knowledge about the resources of the home range, and
especially the sources of food and water during bad
years, is likely to be held by the old females, the only
members of the group that have spent their entire lives

in the home range. In view of this, Rowell (32) has suggested that the often described traveling arrangements of open-country baboons may have been misinterpreted. Observers report that some adult males travel at the head of the column. These males play an "indicator" role as to what routes might be taken, but they do not determine where the group will go. This decision comes from the center of the group where other males walk with adult females and young infants. Another possible way to interpret this is that the decisions are often made by the older females of the dominant genealogies which form the physical and social core of the group. The males with them are the ones most attached to them, often probably their brothers and sons. Breuggeman (5) reports that among the rhesus macaques on Cayo Santiago the primary factor in determining whether a new male will be admitted to the central core of the group is his degree of acceptance by the dominant females. Other evidence to support this comes from six months' observation of a small group of rhesus without an adult male (28). The females of the group continued a normal daily round without disorganization. Eventually, after many months, an adult male from another group was allowed to join up with them, but the daily round continued as before, uninfluenced by the presence of the new male.

Studies on the Indian rhesus macaque and on the Japanese macaque suggest that within the social group genealogies are often ranked. In fact, these studies have come up with the rather startling conclusion that, for a large percentage of the members of these societies, it is sufficient only to know the mother of the individual and its birth order among its siblings, to know its rank in the dominance hierarchy of the group (17, 36). Among these macaques, a young monkey takes its rank directly from its mother, so that dominance relations between young peers are entirely determined by the relative ranks of their mothers. It is easy to understand why this should be so. The mothers respond to a threat to their offspring as if it were to themselves. If the threat comes from an animal ranking above the mother, she may snatch up her infant and flee or give placating gestures. If the threat comes from one ranking below, she will respond aggressively with threats and chases. A young monkey cannot help but learn from these experiences both general social attitudes and the specific treatment due to individuals in the group. At the same time other group members learn that a particular little monkey, no matter how physically insignificant, may have a powerful and aggressive mother to back him up. In groups where genealogies have grown large, a young monkey can count on not only his mother but also his maternal aunts and uncles, his older siblings, perhaps even his cousins, when he needs help. Among Japanese macaques the high-ranking genealogies are likely to be the most cohesive, which seems sensible, since the higher the rank of the genealogy, the more members are likely to directly benefit from their coalitions.

When these young rhesus and Japanese macaques reach full adulthood, there is a split between the social experiences of females and males. Females continue in the routine of life which was established when they were very young. Sexual maturity and motherhood do not alter the bonds and rankings that have already been established. For males, however, the possibility arises at puberty of achieving a rank either above or below their genealogical position through dominance interactions and fights. Even so, it is clear that family connections have a strong influence on the status of males and that young males of the high-ranking genealogies are

more likely to stay in their natal groups and maintain a
high rank (18). Because males may change their rank
through aggressive interactions and because the males
in a group have a relatively high turnover rate, the
male-dominance hierarchy is very unstable compared to
the female hierarchy. For the males of a group, some
changes in their hierarchy are likely to happen every
year, but for females there is little or no change in their
relative statuses even when groups split and genealogies
break off (20, 25).

Ranked genealogies have not been reported for all
terrestrial primates partly because most field studies
have been too short to determine the existence of
genealogies. However, my own field observations of the
vervet monkey suggest that this phenomenon is not
confined to the macaque genus. It is also quite likely
that in some species, like the chimpanzee and many arboreal monkeys, dominance itself plays a much smaller
role in daily life than in the baboons and macaques.
The development of ranked genealogies would be unlikely even though the matrifocal subunit would still
remain the major determinant of activities in the daily
routine of sleeping, feeding, grooming, resting, and play.

In some monkeys, such as vervets, langurs, patas, and
geladas adult females readily band together against individual males in dominance encounters. It is quite
likely that genealogical cores form the nucleus of such
coalitions. For example, in the vervet monkey group I
studied, coalitions were easily formed against the top
three males in the group if they offended the females by
trying to monopolize some concentrated and prized
food source or by frightening an infant. These coalitions were formed irrespective of relative dominance
status so that even females from the lowest genealogies
would chase a male who had made one of their infants
scream. Males who had recently joined the group were

more vulnerable to such attacks than were males belonging to high-ranking lineages, but no males were immune. A typical sequence might begin with a female screaming and soliciting aid by giving rapid glances back and forth between the adult male and the females whose support she sought. The coalition would then attack, running and usually screaming, at the male. The male would turn and flee. He would run as fast as he could until he reached the nearest tree or rock. He would then run up it and turn to face his chasers who threatened from below. After a minute or so of exchanging threats, the females would then move off, perhaps going back to the food or infant which was the cause of the problem. After that the male might be free to join them, but now on their terms and not on his.

Such coalitions of females against a male never seemed to affect the rank of the male concerned. He was never caught or bitten, and even a series of such encounters did not alter his individual rank. However, there is an effect on the male's behavior, if not his rank, because clearly his ability to bully subordinates is curbed. In particular, he learns to be very careful about frightening infants or juveniles, the single most effective way to arouse a coalition against him. Several times after an infant vervet monkey had screamed, all the nearby adult males immediately left the vicinity even though they were innocent of frightening the infant. Apparently the potential of a female coalition against them created enough anxiety to make them leave. Although female vervets do not enhance their own individual social positions by coalitions, they do limit the potential social autocracy of the large, dominant males.

It is important to note that, although the matrifocal genealogy resembles a human family, there are two major differences. First of all, a matrifocal group is really only a system of interactions based on affection, whereas the family is that and more. Monkeys and apes do not define relations so that individuals play roles in the family which involve defined rights and obligations like brother, sister, mother, father, aunt, or uncle. Any behavior pattern which reduces or limits the frequency of interaction between mother and offspring, such as the passing around of infants in langurs, works against the development of a strong genealogy by diffusing the social contacts. In other words, certain behavior patterns can alter the sharpness of focus of the mother-infant bond so that the developing infant will seek social partners among members of the social group who do not belong to his genealogy. The second way in which a matrifocal group differs from the human family is that there is no father. The special binding of an adult male to the female or females with whom he mates is comparatively rare as a major behavior pattern in primate societies and occurs only in very special circumstances.

The mother-infant bond which ramifies to produce a matrifocal subunit represents a major theme in the social organization of monkey and ape societies. Furthermore, its role in human societies may still not be fully appreciated. This bond apparently produces a behavioral potential which can be emphasized or deemphasized according to the needs of the social system and ecological setting of the group. The bond establishes a positive emotional base which endures and provides considerable stability because it binds successive generations to each other.

The Sexual Bond in Primate Societies

In the past much has been made of the mating systems of the nonhuman primates compared to those of humans. There are the old clichés of either the promiscuous primate horde or else the aggressive, dominant male who jealously guards his harem or demands first choice of an estrous female. The field data, however, do not fit this description. In fact, there is no one primate pattern but a wide range of variation in form, from extreme promiscuity to highly exclusive harem systems, from casual mating to highly excited, emotional bonding between mating individuals. Perhaps the best generalization that can be made about primate mating systems is that they tend to be compatible with, or even be a mainstay for, the social system which itself is adapted to meet the demands of the environment (21).

Some of the variation between groups is better understood when the evolutionary strategy of the female as well as the male is analyzed. For the most part, male evolutionary strategy is to mate with as many females as possible without paying too high a price in terms of competition with other males. The problems for a female are very different. She has no difficulty in becoming pregnant. Her strategy involves the raising of as many infants as possible to maturity. For a female, males are a resource in her environment which she may use to further the survival of herself and her offspring. If the environmental conditions are such that the male role can be minimal, a one-male group is possible (33). Only one male is necessary for a group of females if his only role is impregnation. This is why among tree-living monkeys the most common (but not the only) form of social group is composed of one male with several females and their young. Tree-living monkeys do not have the problem of defense from predators in the same way that open-country primates do. In forests, predators do not hunt in groups but rather by stealth, and the best defense against them is to be alert and to stay out on small branches which will not support a large predator. The role of an adult male is minimal in these circumstances and one may be enough for a group of females. As summarized by Eisenberg et al. (9), the number of males in a given group will depend on the advantage of their presence to the reproducing females. In general the more ground-living and open-country the adaptation, the larger the male role will be and the less the likelihood of a one-male mating system. (The only exceptions to this are groups like the patas monkey and the hamadryas baboon, where there has been selective advantage for a minimal-sized foraging unit. Here the advantages of a large, multi-male group in open country have been sacrificed because of the scarceness and poor quality of the food supply.) The more the male role expands in respect to responsibility for vigilance and group protection, the more the leader male needs to take on helpers and share the sexual potential of the females to ensure the survival of his (and the other males') offspring. This analysis from the perspective of the female primate does not deny that there is competition between males for the role of leader male in a one-male group or dominant male in a multi-male group because of the evolutionary advantage that role may carry in respect to impregnation of females. This point of view simply emphasizes that male and female evolutionary strategies can differ even though they belong to the same reproductive system. Neither strategy alone can be used to give a complete analysis of social behavior. Both are equally valid and we ought to consider both in trying to understand a social system and how it works.

The Separation of Roles Between the Sexes

The roles played by males and females vary from species to species among the primates. In a number of primate species there is actually a minimal amount of role differentiation between the sexes beyond the obvious one in which females care for infants because they are equipped to nurse them and males are not. In the more ground-living species both males and females are very much attracted to, tolerant, and protective of young infants. In fact, it is not uncommon among the macaques and baboons for an adult male to "adopt" or take on as a protégé a young, weaned juvenile (5, 26). When special relations form between an adult male and a juvenile, the adult male will groom the youngster, cradle it in his arms when it sleeps, protect it in dominance interactions, and generally play a "maternal" or protective and solicitous role. In some cases in which the genealogies of the individuals are known, the juvenile is often a younger sibling of the adult male who has increased his rate of interaction with it after it was weaned and their mother's attention turned to a new infant. A few cases of adoptions of orphaned, weaned infants are known for chimpanzees, baboons, and rhesus macaques. In these cases the infant was adopted by an older sibling who had been closely attached to the mother before her death. There is no evidence to suggest that inexperienced females are necessarily more fit than inexperienced males in caring for these infants and both sexes are motivated to try.

Among the more tree-living primates, adult males are often aloof from young animals, tolerant of them perhaps, but not drawn to them in the way that males of semiterrestrial and terrestrial species often are. In many of the highly arboreal species the infant is kept very close to its mother for a long period during its early development, and probably the need for any special relationship with adult males is minimal. As mentioned earlier, one of the most common forms of social organization in tree-living primates is a group of one adult male, several females, and their young. The contribution of the male to the group's well-being is minimal and usually consists of impregnation of the females and of occasional aggressive displays toward potential predators. In fact, the male himself is likely to be loosely attached or semiperipheral to the social core of the group. He more or less follows the females and young about, protecting them from other males and perhaps from predators. If the male should die or disappear, the females do not show psychological dependence on him but rather continue their usual rounds undisturbed.

In contrast the roles played by adult males in ground-living and open-country primates are sometimes, but not always, correlated with great sexual dimorphism in body size, weight, muscularity, distribution of hair on the body, and size of canines. The adult male baboon is a prime example of this kind of dimorphism. His body weight is more than double that of an adult female. His shoulders and neck are covered by a thick mane of long hair which helps protect these areas in fights at the same time that it adds to the impression of size and strength. His upper canines are long and razor-sharp, constantly honed by grinding against specially formed teeth on the lower jaw.

However, there is no simple correlation between habitat and sexual dimorphism (see Table 1). Several examples of extreme dimorphism in body size are correlated with arboreal life (proboscis monkey and the orangutan) whereas instances of minimal amounts of dimorphism are found in both tree-living and ground-living species (leaf-eating monkeys, chimpanzees, and humans). This is so because there is usually more than one way to solve a problem posed by the environment. The solution is likely to relate both to the evolutionary history of the species and the adaptive niche it is presently occupying. So, for example, humans and one of our closest relatives, chimpanzees, have minimal development of sexual dimorphism in regards to size and

Species	Body Weight of Female as Per Cent of Male	Habitat
East African baboon	43%	terrestrial
Proboscis monkey	48%	arboreal
Gorilla	48%	arboreal
Orang-utan	49%	terrestrial
Rhesus macaque	69%	semiterrestrial
Indian langur monkey	89%	semiterrestrial
Chimpanzee	89%	terrestrial
Human	89%	terrestrial
Lar gibbon	93%	arboreal

TABLE 1. Percentage relations between the average body weights of fully adult females and males in Old World monkeys, apes, and humans. (After Schultz [39])

strength. In the course of evolution early humans must have moved out from the protection of woodlands into more open country with greater dangers from the group-hunting carnivores. However, this problem was not solved by selecting for adult males twice the size of adult females as in baboons and patas monkeys. Rather, humans responded with a different pattern, the use of weapons and group defense.

In species where dimorphism is minimal, there may be very little difference in aggressive potential between males and females. For example, in the gibbon (the small ape that lives in mated pairs) the body and canine size of males and females is virtually the same. It is not surprising then to learn that female gibbons are highly aggressive and act as partners to their males when defending their territories against intruders. So, too, in Zambia vervet monkey females joined in with the males in driving off neighboring groups who had invaded the territory. In these situations there seemed to be a differentiation between females carrying young infants and females who were not encumbered. These females without infants would join the males while the new mothers would hang back and watch. Sometimes when the monkey group was "mobbing" predators such as pythons or crocodiles, a vervet female with a young infant would pull it off her chest and plop it down near a "babysitter" before running over and joining the others in threatening the predator.

It should be noted that in this discussion of role differentiation between male and female in primate societies there is no mention of major differences in economic or food-getting activities. With few exceptions the adult males and females in a primate group eat the same range of foods in roughly the same percentages, although there are instances where very large males may have some advantages in feeding on fruits or nuts in thick shells because of their stronger jaw muscles or where smaller females can feed at the ends of branches in a fruit tree. The only really important and interesting exception to this is in the case of active hunting for meat by baboons (12) and chimpanzees (40). Many of the terrestrial and semiterrestrial and some of the arboreal monkeys and apes show a marked preference for certain items of protein, such as birds' eggs, grubs, fledgling birds, lizards, and large insects. If they should happen upon them in the course of their food quest, they will eat them with relish. Beyond these, there are special instances in baboons and chimpanzees in which certain group members actually join together and cooperate in catching and eating a relatively large mammal such as a rabbit, a young antelope, or even another species of monkey. These co-operative hunters are often males, even though females clearly like to eat the meat and may even beg for a share. Although there is no indication that meat is a major part of the diet of either baboons or chimpanzees (they probably could give it up altogether with no harm done), nevertheless it represents a very interesting behavioral potential. This is especially so when one considers that in humans the evolution of co-operative hunting by males was an integral part of the earliest human adaptive pattern. The final section of this paper will discuss the evolution of the human pattern in greater detail. For the moment it is only important to note that in most primate species there is practically no separation of food-getting activities on a sexual basis.

The Major Features of the Human Adaptive Pattern

The earliest clear evidence of the human way of life comes from the Australopithecines. The fossil and archaeological record of these creatures gives evidence that in spite of their ape-sized brains they possesed a number of the major features of the human adaptive pattern such as almost fully evolved bipedalism, the making of stone tools, the killing of game, and home bases or campsites. The time span of these early humans was from over 4 million until about 1 million years ago. There are many features of the human adaptive pattern, particularly those involving changes in social life, that do not leave clear evidence in the archaeological record or can only be guessed at from slim clues. Nevertheless, these changes in social life were just as important a part of the emerging human adaptive pattern as were stone tools. We can use our knowledge of the behavior of nonhuman primates as well as the

lives of men living today in a gathering-hunting economy to help reconstruct what these changes might have
been.

Let us take what we know about nonhuman primates
and try to speculate on the most probable behavioral
and social attributes of our ape ancestor. First of all,
we would probably find some important differences in
the behavior of males and females. Primate field data
draw a picture of a comparatively adventurous, wandering male able to form bonds with neighbors and relative
strangers, live comfortably in unfamiliar home ranges,
and vigorously defend new territories if they exist.
These males would have a strong tendency to take up
defense of females and young against outside threat but
they would take no economic responsibility for the well-
being of females and young. Females, in contrast,
would be strongly bonded with their genealogies, so
strongly, in fact, that if an old dominant female left the
group, her genealogy might follow her. However, a female would be unlikely to leave the home range of her
birth, and her interests would be strongly focused on
her offspring and close relatives. A genealogy might
contain three or four generations and consist of both
males and females. High-ranking and often larger
genealogies would form the social core of the group,
and the mature generation of "elders" might be composed of a strongly bonded group of brothers and sisters.
Both males and females would be equally concerned
with questions of dominance and social rank if these
were important ecologically. However, for a number of
reasons, some of which are still unclear, males would be
more likely to achieve a rank which differs from that of
their genealogy, and so the relative rankings among
adult males would remain unstable through time. Females, on the other hand, might maintain stable rank
orders which would endure for long periods, and major

changes might occur only when high-ranking genealogies were decimated by death, disease, or by a skew
in the sex ratio of birth in favor of males. Because of
the stability of their social relations and their attachment to their home ranges, adult females probably
would have much greater knowledge about the resources of their environment than would males and they
might play major roles in group leadership. Individuals
would be largely responsible for feeding themselves,
even infants once they were weaned. Their diet would
consist mainly of vegetables and fruit, but there would
be a definite appetite for animal protein, usually in the
form of insects, small reptiles, young birds, eggs, and
other easily collected items. On occasion some of the
adult males would hunt larger game and often they cooperate in hunting down prey. Sometimes this meat
would be informally shared among group members
nearby at the time. Both males and females used tools
casually, much as wild chimpanzees do today. Tools
would not be skillfully made but would be used in a
wide variety of circumstances.

If the above is a reasonable reconstruction of the behavior of man's ape ancestor in respect to social behavior, then it is clear that many of the essential ingredi-
ents of the human adaptive pattern were foreshadowed
in the behavior of nonhuman primates. The next question is what happened to transform this creature into a
human being. The human adaptive pattern rests on a
fundamental shift in economic and social relations
among members of a social group. This shift was dis-
tinctly human even though it was based on a primate
heritage and foreshadowed in the behavior of our ape
ancestors.

The Division of Labor: Many of the elements of the
human adaptive pattern have now been found to occur

in the behaviors of other primates. In some cases these patterns are focal adaptations even in nonhuman primates, such as the establishment of the matrifocal lineage in many monkey and ape societies. Other crucial elements of the human pattern such as bipedalism, tool-using and tool-making, food-sharing, and co-operative hunting of meat, do occur in nonhuman primates but only as relatively minor behavior patterns and not as key adaptations. These behavioral elements came together in the first humans coupled with a fundamental change in social and economic relations within the group. This new pattern of behavior opened up an unexploited niche for our species—one that must have been relatively protected from competition so that even the small-brained Australopithecines were very successful living in it.

More than anything else the new pattern rested on a unique way of exploiting food resources: gathering and hunting based on a division of labor between adult males and adult females. In nonhuman primates each animal is a separate subsistence unit. Infants may be dependent on their mothers and their groups for protection from other monkeys and the dangers of the environment but, once they are weaned, they must feed themselves. In contrast, weaned human young are dependent on adults not only for protection and security but also for food for many years. Because of this long-term dependence on adults for food, the roles of both male and female humans have greatly expanded and much of their time is spent in activities which provide food for dependent young.

In nonhuman primates, finding food means foraging for fruits, vegetables, grasses, and sometimes insects, eggs, and other sources of animal protein. Our species added to, but did not lose, that gathering pattern when co-operative hunting evolved. Because of the long-term dependence of children, a division of labor must have developed in which the adventurous, wandering male became the hunter and the female developed a less mobile role of gatherer and mother. The home ranges of group-hunting mammals are large compared to foragers like monkeys (38), and hunting can be a dangerous activity demanding skill and concentration. As Brown (6), in a cross-cultural survey of women's work, has so ably pointed out, there are certain activities which cannot be performed by a woman burdened with immature offspring. Child-care responsibilities are only compatible with activities which do not demand long trips from home; with tasks which do not require rapt concentration; and with work which is not dangerous, can be performed in spite of interruptions, and is easily resumed once interrupted (see Chapter IV).

In time past mother's milk was the essential food for infants for the first year or so of life. Normal growth and development depended on it and there was no substitute (even the artificial milks of today are inadequate). Since the care of infants had to fall to females anyway because only they could feed them, it is obvious that care of juveniles as well would come to the women in a gathering-hunting division of labor. Furthermore, hunters cannot be burdened with children. It is impossible to go on a three-day hunting trip which may cover a hundred miles or more and carry an infant with a four-year-old following along behind. With the long years that it takes for the human child to develop and learn adult roles and skills, once gathering and hunting had developed as a major adaptive stance, there was no other way for the division to have evolved except between males and females. There is no need to posit special "killer" or "maternal" instincts in males and females to explain the assignment of these roles.

There have been two very important benefits from

the division of labor. The first is probably the key to early human success long before the evolution of large brains and complex culture. The division of labor provided a flexible system of joint dependence on plant and animal foods (14, 15). It created an effective pattern very different from that of group-living carnivores. A stable and balanced diet was certainly much more likely. Hunting is not necessarily a successful enterprise on a day-to-day basis, and data from modern gatherers and hunters indicate that meat usually constitutes less than 50 per cent of the total diet (24). Carnivore populations are often subject to bad years, but the human gathering-hunting pattern has tremendous flexibility. It can adjust to daily, seasonal, or cyclical fluctuations in food supplies as well as geographical and ecological variants. This system permitted the humans to cover most of the earth without speciating, that is, without having to make major changes in anatomy and behavior in order to maintain an adequate food supply in different ecological settings.

The second advantage of the division of labor was that it marked the first step in specializations in food-getting activities. The tools and the way they were used differed between males and females—the beginning of the evolution of more skilled performances in a variety of tool-making tasks and food quests. For example, the effective use of projectiles such as spears, darts, and arrows takes years of practice. Much of the play of young humans involves the development of skills they will need as adults. If only half the adult repertoire needs to be learned by any one individual, then chances are that the learning of such skills will be more effective.

It should be remembered that the division of labor involves some very complex behavior patterns to make it work. The first of these is a psychology of sharing on a regular basis, not just after the finder of food has been satiated. As was mentioned earlier, in spite of their intelligence, monkeys and apes do not think about the nutritional needs of others. Apes sometimes respond to begging gestures but it would never occur to an ape mother to put something aside for her youngster to be sure it has enough to eat that day. For food sharing and division of labor to really work, food has to be shared especially when times are bad and some foragers come back with nothing and others with just a little. Washburn and Moore (43) suggest that food sharing may have placed a new adaptive force on man—one that selected against groups with overly aggressive and dominant individuals who could not control their own emotions and need to dominate others.

The Human Family: The uniqueness of the human adaptive pattern does not rest on the division of labor alone. Human males do not relate to females and young simply as members of an age-sex class. The human pattern is one in which specific males relate to specific females and their young, taking on special responsibility for their welfare. This special relationship with its special economic and social obligations are summed in the role of "husband-father": a role with no true counterpart among the nonhuman primates. There is no way to prove when this role first appeared, but there are good reasons to think that it was closely linked to the establishment of the division of labor. A division of labor without the role "husband-father" can have some very serious side effects, especially in a small group. Take for example a small group of twenty-five individuals, over half of whom will be immature. Chance alone will cause major skews in the sex ratio among adults. How can a division of labor work in a group of ten adults if two are female and eight are male, or vice versa? This skew could be a disaster during a dry season when the only available food was from hunting. With two males having to provide enough food for eight women and all their children, even if hard times lasted only for a month, the group could lose members through starvation or disease. This kind of skew would happen through chance variation in births or from misfortune and disease. There is an ideal behavioral mechanism which guarantees that the division of labor occurs with reasonably balanced numbers of each sex—the establishment of the role "husband-father." This role assures each female that there is a male hunter in the group to balance the needs of herself and her children. It also assures that extra, unmated hunters will look in neighboring groups for females so that a whole region becomes a pool for finding mates instead of just the local group. Today by far the most common form of family in small gatherer-hunter groups is monogamy (one man-one woman) simply because most men can only really hunt for one child-bearing woman at a time. However, a few men do take on extra wives if they are exceptional hunters or if the second wife is an older widow, no longer bearing children. Generally there is a relative shortage of men because in most human groups (including industrial societies) males have a higher death rate than females from the moment of birth.

The human family represents the bonding of an adult male to a matrifocal unit for economic reasons. However, the bonding itself is not a rational, economic process but rather an emotional one. Important adaptive relationships are not left to simple experience and rational evaluation alone to keep them going but rather they are strongly supported by the emotions. So in humans we find major changes in the relations between the sexes which help to maintain this vital bond. The most basic of these changes is in human sexual activity.

Sexual activity acts as a "social glue," so to speak, not between males and females as a class but between mates. For this to happen, a major change in the reproductive pattern of the species had to occur—the suppression of estrus. Female mammals have special changes in the body and in behavior around the time of ovulation which make them seek mates and make them attractive to males. Estrus in a couple of mature females will bring a chimpanzee group to an orgy of copulations lasting several days in which all the males of the group copulate several times with each estrous female. After that there may be no sexual activity for weeks or months until some other female comes into estrus. What would happen to the division of labor if human females came into estrus? If times are bad and vegetable food scarce, who is going to go hunting if there is an irresistible female in camp? But more important, what happens to the special relationship between mates under these circumstances? The human adaptation has been the suppression of estrus and continuous sexual interest under conscious control in both partners. Even so, vestiges of estrous behavior may still exist if we credit the reports that most human females seem to be more sexually oriented around the time of ovulation, though they may not be conscious of its occurrence. Parallel to this has been changes in the factors that elicit sexual excitement in the human male. A human female does not have to be in estrus to be sexually attractive—instead she has evolved a series of special "sign stimuli" which mark her as sexually exciting all of the time. These special features such as fat pads around the nipples and on the hips and buttocks are unique to the human female compared to other primates and have evolved to take the place of estrous signs in nonhuman primate females. It is interesting to remember that humans are generally not a very sexually dimorphic species. If we take a measure of sexual dimorphism such as body weight, we find that humans have a minimal difference of about 10 per cent between males and females. Height and body-weight dimorphisms usually relate to major differences between the sexes in behavioral potentials for aggression as in the baboon and gorilla. The fossil record suggests that even as far back as the Australopithecines sexual differences in body size and weight were minimal in the human line. Differences in muscularity between men and women is greatly exaggerated in modern society because of the relative inactivity of women. As Brown (6) noted in her cross-cultural review of the assignment of tasks to women, the significant determining factor is compatibility with child care and not differences in strength between the sexes (see also Chapter IV of this book). Thus in many societies carrying burdens or cutting wood are considered to be women's work where as in others they are not. Aside from the minimal 10 per cent development of sexual differences in body size, sexual dimorphism in humans relates to sign stimuli like beards or breasts.

The adaptive advantage, then, of the human family may have first come from the fact that it helped to maintain relatively balanced groups in order that the division of labor could function effectively. In fact, it is difficult to see how a division of labor could have worked if there were no behavioral mechanism to keep a balanced sex ratio in these small groups. A division of labor would be a distinct disadvantage to most groups if the sex ratio were unbalanced, because it could keep many adults from efficient productive activity at certain times of year or in certain areas even though they would still have to be fed. Two women gathering for their children and eight men is just as unsuitable as two men hunting for eight women and their children. There are bound to be times when the group's food supply is inadequate as a result. Gathering requires as much experience and skill as does hunting; once a division of labor has been made it cannot be undone overnight and tasks reassigned.

There is no real archaeological evidence to prove that either a division of labor or a human family system existed for the Australopithecines. We do know for certain that the Australopithecines walked erect, made crude stone tools, had home bases, and hunted some meat for food. We can only guess that the other elements of the adaptive complex (the division of labor and the family) were evolving as well. The division of labor and the family represented major economic and social changes in the common primate pattern, which might explain how the Australopithecines, in spite of their small brains, were able to compete successfully with both their ape relatives and group-hunting carnivores and establish themselves in a new adaptive niche.

The Division of Labor and Modern Society

Millions of years have passed since the special human pattern of social and economic relationships first evolved. The Australopithecine stage of human evolution, marked by small-brained forms and minimal development of culture, ended around a million years ago. The Australopithecines were replaced by a much more advanced form, *Homo erectus*, which was itself replaced by the modern species, *Homo sapiens*. These later forms of humans differed substantially from the Australopithecines in the size of their brains. In less than a million years the human brain tripled in size in conjunction with a tremendous proliferation and elaboration of culture. Nevertheless, human beings were still gatherer-hunters. The earliest known evidence for the domestication of plants comes very late in human history, around 12,000 years ago in Southeast Asia. Even the domestication of plants and animals did not radically change human experience in terms of many aspects of social life. Most humans continued to live in small groups, mainly interacting with well-known individuals, many of whom were kin. The traditional division of labor probably worked well during most of our history. Regardless of whether the economy of a group was based on gathering and hunting, farming, fishing, or manufacturing, as long as fertility was high most of the life of the average woman was spent bearing and raising children.

It is only in the modern societies of today such as Europe, North America, Australia, New Zealand, and Japan where the life expectancy of a woman far outstrips her reproductive years and where most families are being limited to only a few children. These societies are and will be concerned with defining new roles for women. The question remains as to whether man's biological heritage places restrictions on defining these new roles. At this point there seems to be very little real evidence for major unlearned differences in the psychology of male and female primates. Aggression, competitiveness, and dominance striving are not exclusive male attributes in primates, and certainly the ability to form bonds belongs to both sexes. Ability to play maternal roles toward youngsters is also found in both sexes among a number of primate species. In the past there have been many facile generalizations about sex differences in nonhuman primates in aggressive potential, social bonding, sexuality, dominance orientation, and ability to play a maternal role. At the present, however, most of these generalizations seemed to have been based on very inadequate sampling of natural behavior or inadequate sampling of the range of adaptations found in nonhuman primates. There may be major sex differences in certain behavior patterns, e.g., aggressiveness in particular species such as the highly dimorphic baboon, but these differences are not so apparent in other species such as the gibbon. Indeed, the overriding conclusion of more than a decade of primate studies is that each primate species has its own adaptive pattern in terms of the relationship between the sexes, and it is thus impossible to generalize from one species of primate to human beings. Each species is best understood in its own terms—sometimes in contrast to other species and sometimes because of similarities and continuities.

However, there are some very important biologically based needs of human children that must be met if roles for women are to be redefined without serious problems. Anthropologists have made a number of cross-cultural studies on the ways in which different societies raise children. They have documented a wide variety of child-rearing beliefs and techniques; ranging from extremes in authoritarianism to permissiveness, and societies where children are thought of as miniature adults and must work and others where they live in a protected world of play until well past puberty. Healthy, normal children are developed in a variety of contexts according to a number of techniques and beliefs. Nevertheless, there are some aspects of the lives of infants and children that in time past have not varied, and it is only in recent times that departures from these patterns have occurred.

The cutting down of the family to a minimal size has

raised problems in modern societies when divorce,
death, or illness removes one of the spouses from a
family with small children. In the traditional, extended
family such misfortune was only a personal loss to the
individuals involved. In most situations there were other
kin to step in and play the roles of mother or father.
Even in everyday matters there were lots of substitutes
in emotional life. If mother was too busy, there was always grandmother, aunts, or older sisters, all ready to
play the role of mother for a hurt or frightened child. A
child raised in the traditional extended family may
never in his entire childhood be left alone with a
stranger or expected to sleep alone in a dark or strange
room. Because of the nature of lactation, in time past
babies could not be left in a crib and given a bottle
propped on a pillow. They were given, at least, a minimal amount of daily body contact during feeding, and
usually they were given more than that. In gatherer-
hunter societies and many traditional societies today infants are carried on their mother's back and sleep with
their mothers at night. Furthermore, babies were
cared for by their mothers or maternal substitutes and
never by strangers. In terms of emotional development
there is a vast difference between being cared for by a
group of familiar people in a familiar environment such
as mother, her sister, father, and grandmother, and
being cared for by strangers in a daycare center or institution. Infants need emotional security and they get this
before their first year is passed by learning that there
are certain individuals some of whom are always present and ready to play the maternal role. The maternal
role is a demanding one. It can be shared between several individuals, but the role itself demands the same
commitment to the child that the child gives in return—
the formation of an emotional bond. An eight-to-ten-
hour day in a social environment which is crowded, im-

personal, and constantly changing, such as the typical urban daycare center for infants, may produce children who form social bonds only with great difficulty. As the work of Bowlby and others (4) suggests, the ability for human beings to bond and form attachments with each other is established during the first year, and emotional privations during the first year cannot be readily made up later in life.

It should be pointed out that the success of daycare centers in Israel and China may be due to the fact that the personnel are recruited from the same neighborhood or village as the children and there is virtually no staff turnover. Such daycare workers are not professional employees—they are much more likely to be relatives or friends of the families involved and they share a long-term commitment and interest in the children. For young children, the key to finding adequate maternal substitutes is in establishing group care that as closely as possible approximates the social and emotional climate of an extended family.

Modern societies are all moving into an era of social experimentation where new answers are being sought to questions never before posed. It is clear that the world has changed—the growth of science and technology has changed social reality so that the traditional division of labor, so successful for humans in time past, no longer seems to hold much reality or validity. However, the fact that the traditional division of labor will no longer place role restrictions on women does not mean that there are not biologically based, emotional needs of children which still have to be met. An individual woman will no longer spend her entire life playing a maternal role to a long series of children. However, a child still needs to have a small, stable group of individuals on whom he or she can count to play a loving, protective maternal role.

Acknowledgments

The field research on which this paper draws for illustration and insight was supported by a National Science Foundation grant (GS 1414) for the study of vervet monkey social behavior in Zambia, Africa, 1967–69. I would also like to thank T. Rowell of the University of California, Berkeley, and C. S. Lancaster, Tulane University, for helpful discussions and suggestions on some of the ideas found in this paper.

References

1. Altmann, S. A., and J. Altmann, 1970. *Baboon Ecology.* Chicago: University of Chicago Press.
2. Ardrey, R. A., 1970. *The Social Contract.* New York: Atheneum.
3. Boelkins, R. C., and A. P. Wilson, 1972. "Intergroup social dynamics of the Cayo Santiago Rhesus (*Macaca mulatta*) with special reference to changes in group membership by males." *Primates* 13:125–41.
4. Bowlby, John, 1969, 1973. *Attachment and Loss,* Volumes I and II. New York: Basic Books.
5. Breuggeman, J. A., 1973. "Parental care in a group of free-ranging rhesus monkeys (*Macaca mulatta*)." *Folia primatologica* 20:178–211.
6. Brown, J., 1970. "A note on the division of labor by sex." *American Anthropologist* 72:1073–78.
7. Chance, M. E. A., and C. J. Jolly, 1970. *Social Groups of Monkeys, Apes and Men.* New York: E. P. Dutton.
8. DeVore, I., and K. R. L. Hall, 1965. "Baboon ecology." In *Primate Behavior,* I. DeVore, ed., pp. 20–52. New York: Holt, Rinehart.
9. Eisenberg, J. F., N. A. Muckenhirn, R. Rudran, 1972. "The relation between ecology and social structure in primates." *Science* 176:863–74.
10. Gartlan, J. S., and C. K. Brain, 1968. "Ecology and social variability in *Cercopithecus aethiops*," in *Primates: Studies in Adaptation and Variability,* P. Jay, ed., pp. 253–92. New York: Holt, Rinehart.

11. Hall, K. R. L., and I. DeVore, 1965. "Baboon social behavior." In *Primate Behavior; Field Studies of Monkeys and Apes,* I. DeVore, ed., pp. 53–110. New York: Holt, Rinehart.

12. Harding, R. S. O., 1973. "Predation of a troop of olive baboon (*Papio anubis*)." *American Journal of Physical Anthropology* 38:587–91.

13. Hazama, M., 1964. "Weighing wild Japanese monkeys in Arashiyama." *Primates* 5:81–104.

14. Isaac, Glynn, 1968. "Traces of Pleistocene hunters." *Man the Hunter,* R. B. Lee and I. DeVore, eds., Chicago: Aldine.

15. Isaac, Glynn, 1971. "The diet of early man: aspects of archaeological evidence from lower and middle Pleistocene sites in Africa." *World Archaeology* 2:278–99.

16. Kaufman, I. C., 1973. "The role of ontogeny in the establishment of species-specific patterns." *Early Development* 51:381–97.

17. Kawamura, S., 1958. "Matriarchial social ranks in the Minoo-B troop: a study of the social rank system of Japanese monkeys." *Primates* 1:149–56.

18. Koford, C., 1963. "Ranks of mothers and sons in bands of rhesus monkeys." *Science* 141:356–57.

19. Koford, C., 1966. "Population changes in rhesus monkeys: Cayo Santiago, 1960–1964." *Tulane Studies in Zoology* 13:1–7.

20. Koyama, N., 1970. "Changes in dominance rank and division of a wild Japanese monkey troop in Arashiyama." *Primates* 11:335–91.

21. Kummer, H., 1971. *Primates Societies: Group Techniques of Ecological Adaptation.* Chicago: Aldine.

22. Lawick-Goodall, J. van, 1971. *In the Shadow of Man.* New York: Houghton Mifflin.

23. Lindburg, D. G., 1969. "Rhesus monkeys: Mating season mobility of adult males." *Science* 166:1176–78.

24. Lee, R. B., and I. DeVore, 1968. "Problems in the study of hunters and gatherers," in *Man the Hunter,* R. B. Lee and I. DeVore, eds., pp. 3–13. Chicago: Aldine.

25. Missakian, E. A., 1972. "Genealogical and cross-genealogical dominance relations in a group of free-ranging rhesus monkeys (*Macaca mulatta*) on Cayo Santiago." *Primates* 13:169–81.

26. Mitchell, G. D., 1969. "Paternal behavior in primates." *Psychological Bulletin* 71:399–417.

27. Morris, D., 1970. *The Human Zoo.* New York: McGraw-Hill.

28. Neville, M. K., 1968. "A free-ranging rhesus monkey troop lacking adult males." *Journal of Mammalogy* 49:771–73.

29. Paterson, J. D., 1973. "Ecologically differentiated patterns of aggressive and sexual behavior in two troops of Ugandan baboons, *Papio anubis.*" *American Journal of Physical Anthropology* 38:641–48.

30. Ransom, T. W., 1971. *Ecology and Social Behavior of Baboons in the Gombe Stream National Park.* Ph.D. dissertation, University of California, Berkeley.

31. Rowell, T. E., 1967. "Variability in the social organization of primates." In *Primate Ethology*, D. Morris, ed., pp. 219–35. Garden City, New York: Doubleday.

32. ———, 1969. "Long-term changes in a population of Ugandan Baboons," *Folia primatologica* 11:241–54.

33. ———, 1974. "Contrasting adult male roles in different species of nonhuman primates." *Archives of Sexual Behavior* 3:143–49.

34. Saayman, G. S., 1971. "Behavior of the adult males in a troop of free-ranging chacma baboons (*Papio ursinus*)." *Folia primatologica* 15:36–57.

35. Sade, D. S., 1965. "Some aspects of patent-offspring and sibling relations in a group of rhesus monkeys, with a discussion of grooming." *American Journal of Physical Anthropology* 23:1–18.

36. ———, 1967. "Determinants of dominance in a group of free-ranging rhesus." In *Social Communication Among Primates*, S. A. Altmann, ed., pp. 99–114. Chicago: University of Chicago Press.

37. Schaller, G., 1963. *The Mountain Gorilla.* Chicago: University of Chicago Press.

38. ———, and G. Lowther, 1969. "The relevance of carnivore behavior to the study of early hominids." *Southwestern Journal of Anthropology* 25:307–41.

39. Schultz, A. H., 1969. *The Life of Primates.* London: Weidenfeld and Nicolson.

40. Teleki, G., 1973. *The Predatory Behavior of Wild Chimpanzees.* Lewisburg, Pennsylvania: Bucknell University Press.

41. Tiger, L., 1969. *Men in Groups*. New York: Random House.
42. ———, and R. Fox, 1971. *The Imperial Animal*. New York: Holt, Rinehart.
43. Washburn, S. L., and R. Moore, 1974, *Ape into Man*. Boston: Little, Brown, and Co.
44. Wickler, W., 1974. *The Sexual Code*. New York: Doubleday/Anchor.

III. BIOLOGICAL INFLUENCES ON SEX DIFFERENCES IN BEHAVIOR

ASHTON BARFIELD

There is abundant folklore about the behavioral distinctions between men and women. Women are frail, passive, undersexed, moody, intuitive talkers—men are strong, aggressive, highly sexed, stable, rational doers. How genuine are the differences? How much does biology contribute to the dichotomy? Let us begin by examining the strictly biological differences, and then pass to an examination of several areas of behavior. At the very beginning, there is . . .

Embryonic Development

The individual's sex is determined at the moment of conception, when the egg, with an X chromosome, is united with the sperm, which carries either an X or a Y chromosome. The fertilized eggs with XX are females; those with XY are males. In the normal sequence of events, XX embryos will develop ovaries containing potential eggs, a female reproductive tract, and external genitals consisting of a clitoris and two pairs of skin folds. Embryos with XY genetic constitution will acquire testes with potential sperm, a reproductive tract and its glands, and external genitals composed of the penis and scrotal sac (52).

In this limited space, the huge number of pertinent scientific studies cannot be discussed in detail. Therefore, reported sex differences are generally treated as if they are of equal magnitude. Studies of dubious validity are either not cited, or are presented with the necessary qualifications. To keep the bibliography to a manageable size, the reader is referred to review articles wherever possible.

These reproductive differences between the sexes develop over four to five months. Until the seventh week after conception, the only distinguishing characteristic is genetic (52). Both sexes contain undifferentiated gonads, both types of reproductive tract, and undifferentiated external genitals. The XY genetic constitution will usually cause the gonad to develop into a testis. The embryonic testis will begin to secrete *androgens,* the male sex hormones, which will cause the male tract and glands to develop, and the female tract to disappear. Androgens will also cause the small external projection, the genital tubercle, to elongate into a penis, and the genital folds to fuse into a scrotum. In the XX embryo, the gonad becomes an ovary. It does not produce androgens, nor, at this stage, *estrogens* and *progestins,* the female sex hormones. In this absence of hormonal stimulation, female development proceeds. The female tract differentiates while the male tract disappears. The genital tubercle remains small, as the clitoris, and the genital folds remain unfused (3).

This bipotentiality of the sexes has been demonstrated by experiments in subhuman mammals. If the female is exposed to the influence of androgens during this fetal period, structural development will proceed along male lines. Conversely, if the male is deprived of androgenic influence, a female system will be produced (89). In humans, accidents of development occasionally yield similar aberrations (89), showing that the same bipotentiality exists in our own species. Therefore, genetic differences can only predispose; they cannot guarantee the development of the appropriate reproductive structures.

In addition to differences associated with the reproductive tract, differentiation between the sexes occurs in the brain. The *hypothalamus,* located at the base of the brain, controls the release of hormones by the *pituitary* gland next to it; these pituitary hormones influence the gonads' production of gametes (eggs or sperm) and sex hormones. In the adult male, there is a pattern of continuous pituitary hormone release, resulting in a steady output of sperm and androgens. In the adult female, there is both a low level of continuous pituitary hormone release and a periodic burst of pituitary hormones; this combination causes cyclic production of eggs, estrogens, and progestins. Animal experiments suggest that there are two separate brain control centers for the periodic and continuous patterns, and that fetal androgens cause permanent inhibition of the periodic center in the male (89).

In animals, androgens can also act on the fetal brain to influence sexual behavior (89). Normal adult male rats do not manifest feminine reproductive behavior, even when injected with female hormones. Normal adult female rats show predominantly feminine reproductive behavior; although they do occasionally mount other animals, this behavior cannot be markedly increased by male hormones. However, manipulation of the hormones during development can have pronounced effects on adult behavior. If male rats are not exposed to androgens during a certain developmental period, they will engage less in masculine mating behavior as adults—even if androgens are administered in the adult stage. Furthermore, such males will actually show feminine mating behavior if they receive female hormones. Conversely, developing female rats exposed to androgens will show marked reduction or absence of feminine sexual behavior as adults, even with female sex hormone administration. Moreover, they will display more of the masculine behavioral pattern than normal females, particularly following androgen treatment. The evidence again points to the existence of two separate brain centers in each individual, with androgens

inhibiting the feminine center. (There are subtle differences among various mammalian species concerning
which sex(es) manifest(s) both types of reproductive
behavior (124), but none of this variation contradicts
the theory of two separate behavioral centers.)

Not only does development in the rat proceed in this
sequence—from gonad through reproductive tract, external genitals, neural control of gonadal function, and
behavior—but there is also a limited period during
which each system is susceptible to masculinization
(89). Later administration of androgens cannot com-
pensate for androgen deficiency during development of
a system. The same developmental sequence occurs in
human embryos, and the same bipotentiality is known
to exist for human gonadal structure, reproductive tract,
external genitals, and brain control of gonadal functioning (89). Moreover, since androgen levels in the male
human embryo do remain higher than those in the female until long past the time of genital differentiation
(1), the timing is appropriate for an influence on the
developing brain.

Physical Traits

Sex differences are apparent even at birth. Males are
slightly longer and heavier (34). Females have a
lower percentage of total body weight in muscle, and,
very soon, a greater proportion of fat (101). Female
lungs and heart are proportionally smaller than those of
males (22).

During the first eight years after birth, boys and girls
have similar hormone levels (13) and similar physical
development, though the minor initial differences are
maintained. With puberty and large-scale secretion of
sex-appropriate hormones, these differences become

more pronounced. The growth spurt begins later in the typical male, then proceeds at a faster rate for a longer time, thereby widening the gap in height (79). Growth differences cause females to have lighter skeletons, different shoulder/pelvis proportions, different pelvic bone shapes, and different socket shapes at the shoulder and hip (32). The relative proportion of fat to total body weight increases in the female, but decreases in the male (79). All these differences contribute to such feminine characteristics as less strength, less endurance for heavy labor, more difficulty in running or overarm throwing, and better ability to float.

These relative differences in secondary sex characteristics occur in all cultures, but there are important limitations. For instance, they hold true only within a particular population; the females of one group will not necessarily be smaller or fatter than the males of every other group. In addition, the magnitude of the average difference between the sexes varies from population to population; females and males of some groups will resemble each other much more than they do in other groups (21). Furthermore, environment and culture greatly influence the extent of these physical differences. Good nutrition and physical activity enhance size and muscularity. Practice improves the ability to perform particular skills; the amount of practice will, in turn, be a function of the societal pressures to perform, or not to perform, a particular act. The effect of culture can also be far more subtle. If an individual's physical traits place him/her at either end of the usual range of traits, the individual is likely to be treated as particularly representative or unrepresentative of his/her gender. Since expectations of behavior help to produce that very behavior, ultimately the individual will probably perform in a manner appropriate to his/her physical type.

Physiological Characteristics

One of the earliest differences between the sexes is the faster maturation rate shown by females, perhaps as early as the seventh week of embryonic life (52). After five months of pregnancy, females are two weeks ahead of males; at birth, they are four weeks ahead. Females complete most processes earlier, including the acquisition of skills such as walking, talking, and bladder and bowel control (117). They also attain the peaks of certain characteristics sooner, including puberty and full physiological maturity.

Males are more susceptible than females to physical disorders, disease, and death (99). During the first year of life, one third more males die, primarily from infectious diseases (34). The male death rate continues to be higher at other ages. Moreover, as a population acquires an increased life expectancy, this benefit appears to be greater for women than for men, although this may simply represent the reduction of deaths connected with pregnancy and birth (99).

Some diseases are directly related to the X chromosome. Since males have only one X chromosome, they have no opportunity to mask the harmful recessive genes that produce color-vision defects, blood-clotting disorders, or deficiencies in immunity (44). Although it is true that one X chromosome is inactivated in females, this inactivation is apparently not complete for all genes (52). In addition, it seems that either X chromosome may be inactive in different cells of the same individual (93).

Males also seem to be more prone to such speech defects as stuttering and language disorders, to reading disabilities, to limited vision, to hardness of hearing and deafness, and to mental defectiveness (34). Since maturation is a particularly vulnerable period for the development of such disorders, the prolonged maturation process which characterizes males may contribute to their greater susceptibility.

The medical symptoms of psychological stress appear to vary for men and women. Men exhibit peptic ulcers and skin disorders, whereas women experience headaches, migraines, backaches, and insomnia (33). Suicide, a behavioral symptom of psychological stress, also shows a sex differential. More females attempt suicide, but more males succeed (99). Some studies report that the characteristic types of mental illness differ. Men have a higher incidence of schizophrenic and obsessive-compulsive disorders, while women manifest more manic and depressive emotional psychoses (33). However, this division may reflect various cultural influences. For instance, if a particular mental illness is more socially acceptable for one sex, less pains will be taken by that sex to hide it. Moreover, high frequency of a particular illness in one sex may cause expectation—and disproportionately high or even mistaken diagnosis—of its occurrence. On the other hand, the less frequent a particular condition, the more likely it is to be labeled "illness" when it does occur. And finally, the different types of childhood training or adult situations experienced by the two sexes may result in different types of maladjustments.

Other disabilities to which males are more prone may be due to typically masculine activities. For example, since males are generally more active, they have more accidents, injuries, and violent deaths. More males smoke cigarettes, and their incidence of lung cancer is higher. Females, it should be noted, are closing the gaps in both categories (99). Biological predisposition and social factors can interact in subtle ways. Men's stressful occupations are considered to contribute to their higher incidence of heart disease and stomach ulcers. However, women with premature cessation of female hormone secretion also seem to have an increased risk of heart disease—and the earlier the hormonal cessation, the greater the risk (122). Another example is even more complex: though there are more American women than men who are obese, the men are more susceptible to such consequences of excessive weight as strokes, diabetes, and pneumonia (99). A key question here is whether this is due to the difference in activities and stress, or to some fundamental propensity.

To summarize briefly, differing environments can contribute to the relative prevalence of certain diseases in the sexes. An additional factor may be the willingness to admit that a particular disorder exists, which could result in a higher apparent incidence. It could also lead to more prompt treatment, thus reducing the incidence of subsequent or associated disorders. Still, it does appear that males are genuinely somewhat more vulnerable than females to physical problems. More males die very young, long before activities diverge along sexual lines (99). Moreover, a study (78) of men and women living in religious cloisters with very similar diets, housing, medical care, occupations, and work and sleep patterns, showed that the females still survived better at every age, even though both sexes had above-average life expectancies. Interestingly, the females were just as prone to infectious diseases; it was in degenerative diseases that they fared better.

It is also known that some basic physiological processes are slightly different in the two sexes. Even in infancy, the male metabolic rate is higher (34), although it has been claimed (14) that this difference is not significant. From the age of two months on, males consume more calories (53). Adult males have a lower resting heart rate, higher blood pressure, greater oxygen-carrying capacity, and more efficient recovery from muscular activity (53). These factors contribute to the male capacity for heavy and prolonged muscular exertion. Of course, regular and vigorous exercise in females will enhance these same qualities, though it may not eliminate the sex differences in their entirety.

Certain sensory differences have been reported. From birth on, females are more sensitive to touch and to pain (53). Though there are no sex differences in hearing at birth (66), adult females seem to have more acute hearing (perhaps only for the higher sound frequencies), and better ability to locate the source of a sound (34). There are no differences in active visual behavior at birth, although newborn females are more responsive than males to light (66). The information on adult visual differences is far from conclusive, since there are reports that males have better (34), equal, (34) or worse (18) visual ability. Newborn females are more receptive to sweet-tasting stimuli (66). Adult females may be more sensitive to bitter and sour tastes, but the evidence on both taste and smell discrimination in adults is quite contradictory (34).

Another area of physiological sex differences is the adult secretion of gonadal hormones. It is misleading to speak of the various gonadal hormones as sex-specific, since androgens, estrogens, and progestins are all secreted in *both* females and males. There are substantial differences, however, in the actual levels of these hormones, the sensitivity to particular hormones, the sources (gonads versus adrenals), and the pattern of secretion. In the male, androgen secretion is continuous. In contrast, the female shows pronounced rhythmic hormonal fluctuations during the menstrual cycle. (See Figure 1). During the first half of the cycle, estrogens are secreted in increasing amounts. After ovulation, during the second half of the cycle, the ovary secretes small amounts of estrogens and more progestins. In the last few days before menstruation, hormonal secretion falls off precipitously. Other physiological characteristics fluctuate with the menstrual cycle. After ovulation, there

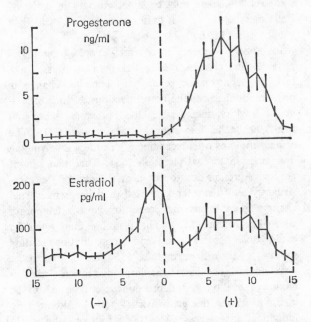

DAYS FROM LH PEAK (=OVULATION)

Figure 1. Progesterone and estradiol mean levels in daily samples obtained from ten women during ovulatory cycles. The day of the peak levels of luteinizing hormone (i.e. approximately the day of ovulation) is the reference day. The vertical bar at each point represents one standard error of the mean. (Adapted from Daniel R. Mishell, Jr., et al., "Serum gonadotropin and steroid patterns during the normal menstrual cycle," *American Journal of Obstetrics and Gynecology* III, pp. 60–65 [1971])

are slight rises in the temperature and metabolic rate of red blood cell turnover (115), and allergic sensitivity (113). Sensitivity to detection of touch, sound, taste, and smell stimuli may decrease, whereas visual sensitivity seems to rise (23, 51, 114). In the few days prior to menstruation, there may be slight changes in carbohydrate metabolism and/or fluid retention, and/or a slight weight gain (115).

In some women, there are more pronounced physiological changes during this premenstrual period, including constipation, change in appetite, change in pigmentation, susceptibility to infections, asthma, blood-vessel fragility, increase in blood pressure, aches and pains, headache, and neurological seizures (20). The same symptoms often accompany disorders involving an imbalance in adrenal secretion (55). Since that sort of adrenal secretion does occur near the end of the menstrual cycle, it has been proposed that the premenstrual changes in estrogens and progestins cause a temporary adrenal imbalance (55). The resulting fluid retention could cause tissue swelling and blood dilution, leading to many of the other symptoms (55). In addition to the physiological changes, behavioral disruptions such as anxiety, hostility, and depressions are reported to be common during the premenstrual period. Although no individual experiences all of the symptoms, the whole group of changes has been collectively referred to as the *premenstrual syndrome*. It has been suggested that the behaviorial changes could result directly from the adrenal changes, or indirectly from the fluid retention (55).

Behavior

We have seen that there are certain biological differences between the sexes which might account for differences in behavior. Now let us examine some examples of behavior to see whether differences are indeed found, and if so, what is known about possible biological influences. The logical place to begin is with the newborn, before there has been any opportunity for cultural factors to come into play.

1. Newborns and Infants

In the first few days after birth, males and females show roughly equal amounts of total activity, but the specific behaviors vary. Female movements tend to be finer and more restricted, consisting of twitching of the lips, smiling, sucking, and raising of the brows (53). Males show more gross, vigorous bodily motion such as startles and sudden convulsive movements. Although the male raises his head higher and is stronger (66), it is possible that the large body movements are less indicative of greater strength than of his relatively less developed nervous system.

It has been reported that infant males are more fretful and irritable than females (53); they fuss more and are more difficult to calm (90). But this may not be entirely innate. It could be initially influenced by circumcision, which is usually performed within the first four days (66). It is also clear that differential treatment by the mother begins early. Mothers look at, stimulate, and pacify male infants more (53). But this in turn may be directly related to the differences in infant behavior. In a study of kibbutz infants (37), where sex differences in treatment are deliberately minimized, males took far longer to finish feeding and had more frequent diaper changes. The result was a large increase in total caretaking time for males. Even if males are not inherently more fretful, the increased amount of caretaking may set up expectations in the male infant which lead to such behavior; thus, the behavioral difference would be an indirect effect of a biological difference. Another study (90) showed that mothers used more preventive attention for males, and that females often quieted themselves. It has also been found that males are more restless before feeding and more tranquil after feeding, whereas the opposite is true in females (118).

A few sex differences at birth in responses to auditory or visual stimuli have been reported (66). For example, while both sexes respond more to the cry of another baby than to an artificially produced sound of the same intensity, females appear to be more responsive than males (53). Soon after birth, further quantitative and qualitative differences emerge in both auditory and visual behavior. Females pay more attention to auditory sequences than to visual patterns, while the converse is true of males (53). At three months, females will look longer at photographs of faces than at drawings of normal or distorted faces. Males fail to discriminate between these types of stimuli, but still spend more time looking at all types. Females also vocalize more than males in response to the stimuli (34). In the males, the amount of time spent looking is related to the amount of time awake, perhaps representing an endogenous attribute. In the females, the amount of time spent looking is correlated with the amount of maternal stimulation and face-to-face interaction (90). Attempts to condition a certain behavior pattern require an auditory reward for females and a visual reward for males (34). This is reportedly consistent for all later ages, including adults (54). Five- to six-month-old females pay more attention to photographs or drawings of human faces, whereas males fix more on geometric forms, preferably complex or novel ones (34).

These results have been cited as evidence that 1) males are more visually oriented, 2) females are more auditorily oriented, and 3) since female visual and auditory responses are strongly influenced by social stimuli, females are predisposed to social interaction. But differences in treatment do occur. While male infants are touched more, female infants are talked to and smiled at more (66). Female vocalizations are imitated more often, even though males vocalize as much (90). Parents will spend more time trying to get females to smile or to vocalize than they will with males, in spite of the fact that there is no difference in infant performance of these tasks (90). Thus, stereotyped sex-role attitudes are introduced very early. It has also been reported that male infants sleep longer (90) (although this is not found in all studies [37]). More sleep might result in less exposure of the male to both social and sensory stimuli.

The consensus seems to be that there is a slight potential for different behavior patterns, but the differences are variable, and the overlap is so extensive that the behaviors are not sufficient to characterize males or females (66, 90). In interviews of mothers (111), most have expressed the idea that males and females should be treated differently. However, they also frequently stated that their actions toward infants were different because of the child's gender-appropriate behavior, rather than as an attempt to cause it. For example, it has been suggested that because the male is less developed, he is more prone to physical distress and is thus more irritable. This would lead initially to more maternal attention, thereby simultaneously reinforcing his own attention-getting behavior and confirming parental expectations of sex-typed behavior—and so on in a circular fashion (90). It certainly seems that both internal and external environments differ quite early for males and females, and that these differences can predispose the development of behavior patterns.

2. Children and Adults

General Comments: It should already be clear that neither biology nor socialization is the sole determinant of human behavior. As development proceeds, the two interact to produce a complex web. Only occasionally can one discern clear contributions from either. Since experimentation on humans is usually either difficult or unethical, information must be sought in other ways—in studies of subhuman primates, human biological aberrations, the social environment, and other cultures.

Behavioral comparisons are often made between humans and other primates. If such comparisons are reliably based, information about sex differences within particular primate groups might be applicable to humans. However, there are a number of important qualifications. Human observers of animals are most likely to detect and accurately interpret relevant clues in species more closely related to themselves (123). Moreover, primate males and females (like lower mammals) show considerable overlap in behavior, with degrees of "masculine" and "feminine" behavior in any individual (118). Also, the protracted maturation period, and the propensity to learn, permit adaptation to a considerable variety of situations (123). For instance, it appears that much of the social behavior of primates is strongly influenced by the habitat (56, 35). Groups living in more varied environments generally show greater variations in behavior, and a wider range of adaptation to local conditions (56). Because such flexibility can exist within a species, it is difficult to be confident of extrapolations from subhuman primates to humans.* Further difficulties arise from observations of captive animals, in whom extreme behavior patterns often emerge (35). However, with these cautions in mind, we can consider some aspects of primate behavior for clues to sex differences in human behavior.

Direct information from humans is also obtainable. Developmental accidents do occur which can provide an equivalent to experiments. There are instances in which females have been born with masculinized external genitals, either because the mother was treated with progrestins to prevent premature delivery, or because of an adrenal tumor in the fetus which led to excess production of androgens (89). Since the adrenal malfunction can be curbed after birth, no further masculinization need occur. Thus, this type of female (*adrenogenital syndrome*) can be studied for the effects of androgenic exposure limited to the fetal period. Of course, the cultural environments of such individuals may be atypical; doctors and families devote special attention to their condition in general, and their genitals in particular. (Corrective surgery may be necessary.) Therefore, biological variation may not be the only factor involved.

There are other instances of developmental accidents, either of genital masculinization in females or lack of it in males. But in many of these cases, the genitals were more similar to those of the opposite sex, which led to the opposite gender assignment at birth. Consequently, the type of rearing was in the same direction as the biological (hormonal) deviation, and one cannot distinguish the relative contributions of the two factors. In the few cases in which gender of rearing and gender of genitals (usually ambiguous) were in conflict, the focus of the reports (89) has been on the gender identity—

---

* See the excellent chapter by Lancaster in this book.

the sex to which the patient feels (s)he belongs. Extensive studies of the general behavior of these individuals do not exist.

Other information about sex differences in behavior can be obtained from sociological studies of the differences in the way individuals are treated, or regarded (another form of treatment). Children soon learn to distinguish gender, and which characteristics are gender-appropriate (26). Since Chapter V deals with this area, sociological considerations will be introduced only occasionally in this chapter.

Information about the gender differences in other cultures can also give insight into the rarity or universality of various behavioral differences. Although most societies have a division of activities along sex lines, the specific assignment appears to be arbitrary in many cases. Examples of qualities which have been assigned, at some point, to either sex are: vulnerability and the need for cherishing; self-ornamentation; need for a dowry to attract a spouse; role of gossip; and role of burden-bearer or outdoor worker (80). The relevant biological sex differences are not conspicuous in childhood; children must be trained to their future roles (7). Chapter IV discusses the relation of sex roles and economic mode. Other anthropological findings will be mentioned where pertinent in this chapter.

Aggression and Mood

It is widely believed that human aggression is inevitable, particularly in males. This view is based on earlier observations that animal groups were organized around a dominant male who gained his status by defeating the other males. This social structure was considered adaptive for food-gathering, reproduction, and population dispersal and control (123). In a wide variety of vertebrates, brain areas responsible for aggressive behavior have been described, attesting to the perpetuation of a biological basis for such behavior (123, 92). Now, however, there is strong evidence that territorial displays and dominance hierarchies are not very important in many mammalian species, particularly in noncaptive animals (35, 4, and see especially Chapter II of this book). In primates, the role of these factors in natural selection is also dubious, since dominance is not related to reproductive success and is not heritable (4).

Furthermore, aggressive behavior is more modifiable than originally suspected. It is influenced by previous encounters, rearing, and amount of fighting experience (53). Even in the cat, aggression depends upon the specific environment. Escape may be opted for; moreover, if attack occurs, its direction and intensity depend on environmental cues (123). In primate groups where hierarchies exist, the individual's position in the hierarchy is learned. A factor in the learning process is the extent to which the mother supports the infant in aggressive encounters (123). Young male baboons repeat their rough-and-tumble play from infancy, gradually acquiring experience in aggressive behavior (44). If young males associate in infancy with the dominant males at the center of the band, they are more aggressive than baboons raised on the periphery (26). When given electrical stimulation in the aggression area of the brain, monkeys will attack if their social position is dominant, but will cower if it is subordinate (123). Besides such intragroup modification, considerable diversity can be seen from group to group within the same species; in general, the more severe the habitat, the greater the male aggressiveness (35, 68).

It is possible that prenatal androgens have some influence on primate aggressiveness. In young rhesus monkeys, the two sexes show different frequencies of aggressive behavior. The male is more likely to use large muscles and to chase other young animals (67). A male castrated at birth develops higher levels of these behaviors than does the normal female, though not so high as those of the normal male (40). If a pregnant female is injected with an androgen for twenty-five to fifty days, her female offspring will show genital masculinization, and aggressive behavior which is intermediate between normal female and male levels (98). It could be argued that the sex difference in aggressiveness is entirely cultural, attributable to the rhesus mother's differential treatment of offspring according to their apparent sex. The male infant and the mother show greater independence of each other in the early weeks of life, with the mother becoming increasingly punitive to the male, carrying and cradling him less, and directing more of her own total behavior toward the environment (57). Yet it may be that this difference in maternal treatment is produced by the difference in infant behavior—rhesus males at three months are rougher with their mothers than females are (57). Still, the mother does appear to recognize biological sex differences; rhesus mothers frequently inspect and handle the genitals of male infants, while female genitals are examined only once or twice (105). Presumably, a rhesus mother would assume a pseudohermaphroditic female to be male, and treat it accordingly. Nevertheless, the cultural differences in maternal treatment cannot fully explain sex differences in rhesus infant behavior. Even infants raised with only inanimate, cloth-and-wire substitute mothers exhibit sex differences in threat and aggressive play patterns (48). Similarly, prenatally masculinized females taken from their mothers and reared in the nursery still show an increase over normal females in the amount of masculine behavior (97). It is likely that, in normal rhesus monkeys, the differences in both infant behavior and maternal behavior reinforce and augment each other in the production of sex-typed aggressive patterns.

In American children, sex differences emerge by the age of two and a half years in both total amount and type of aggression shown. Although there is considerable overlap, on the average boys display aggression more physically and destructively, whereas girls exhibit verbal or disobedient aggression. Boys also initiate aggression more frequently and retaliate more often, thereby prolonging the aggressive encounter (53). As children develop, both sexes shift toward more verbal, nonphysical modes of aggression, with males lagging behind in this trend (111). In a test situation, males also mete our harsher punishments, particularly if the recipient is another male (53). There is very limited information about aggressiveness in humans who have had aberrant prenatal androgen levels. Most studies (89, 29) of human females with genital masculinization have measured rough outdoor play and found that it is increased in such patients. But specific measures of aggression have not been made. Ehrhardt and Baker (29) have reported that a preliminary analysis of their group of adrenogenital children does not indicate an increase in fighting in the males. The data for the females have not yet been analyzed.

The sex differences in aggressive behavior in children are consistent with training differences. Indeed, one area of great distinction in parental treatment is in more permissiveness for male aggression (111). In a test situation in which both sexes were rewarded for aggressive behavior, sex differences were eliminated (87). In the punishment test situation mentioned earlier, the aggressiveness of females increased with time (54).

The sex distinctions in aggressive behavior observed in American children have been described for other cultures. In most societies (as in the United States), the emphasis in female rearing is on obedience and responsibility, while male rearing focuses on self-reliance (21). There are exceptions which illustrate the influence of the rearing pattern. In the Mundugumor of New Guinea, children of both sexes are encouraged from birth to be self-assertive. In adulthood, both males and females are equally independent, vigorous, and hostile (80). In the Arapesh, both sexes are treated with extreme nurturance, and both are passive as adults (80). However, gender-typed rearing may not necessarily account for all instances of variation in aggressive behavior. In Israeli kibbutzim, where sex stereotypes are de-emphasized, some of the differences still arise between ages one and five (21). Also, in some cultures, children of three to six years show larger differences than do children of seven to ten years, despite a shorter period of socialization (21). These two examples suggest that factors other than gender-typing may have an effect.

Thus, it remains possible that individuals are somewhat more likely to engage in aggression if exposed prenatally to androgens. Hamburg and Lunde (44) have suggested mechanisms for such an effect of androgens: they might facilitate the learning of aggressive behavior by increasing the sensitivity to certain stimuli, such as threat or rough contact; they might also make certain patterns of action, such as large muscle movements, more rewarding, and thereby increase the likelihood of their performance.

Postnatal androgens appear to be of only limited importance for aggressiveness in the rhesus monkey. Fights among adult males, although fierce, are less frequent than fights among females (26). Castration of an adult male may lead to a decrease in aggressiveness, but this depends upon previous fighting experience.

Androgen administration to subordinate males (92), prenatally masculinized females (27), or normal females (98) does not increase aggressiveness or improve status. Androgenic influence is apparently greater during rhesus "childhood," when aggressive patterns are being established. Administration of an androgen to juvenile males can increase their level of aggression (92), whereas males castrated at birth have lower levels than normal males (40). Infant females given an androgen for eight months show an increase in aggressive behavior, and are socially dominant over most males of the same age; the latter phenomenon is undoubtedly facilitated by the treated female's increase in body weight and muscle mass (above the normal male levels), and the precocious acquisition of an adult coat (58).

Another type of aggressive behavior frequently observed in primates is "parental" aggression, in which the young are defended from predators or even from members of the same troop (92). Since this occurs in both sexes, androgens are unlikely to be an important factor.

Studies of aggressiveness or hostility and androgen levels in men have generally shown no correlation for most individuals (24). Although castration will reduce the aggression due to sexual offenses, it does not seem to affect other types of aggression (82). It is very difficult to evaluate reports of the anti-aggression effects of castration, anti-androgens, estrogens, or progestins (92); most of the studies had no controls, and a placebo effect cannot be ruled out.

There has been considerable publicity concerning the extra Y chromosome condition (XYY) and the aggressiveness alleged to accompany it. Unfortunately, there are very few reliable studies, and these have been confined largely to men in institutions (mental or penal), who represent only 10 to 15 per cent of all

XYY individuals (12). The XYY condition is not associated with higher androgen levels (82). Moreover, although XYY men do seem to have abnormal aggressiveness, their criminal behavior is no more violent than that of their fellow inmates. Indeed, they commit more crimes against property and slightly fewer crimes against persons (82). Particularly noteworthy is a comparison with the XXY male, who has an extra X chromosome and low androgen levels. Such individuals are found in roughly the same proportions as XYY men in both the general population and in mental and penal institutions, and commit the same types of crime (82).

There is another area in which biological factors are considered to play a role in aggression. It has been reported that women are more hostile during the premenstrual period, and that this increase in hostility is part of a "premenstrual syndrome" encompassing other behavioral changes such as anxiety and moodiness. Females often report in interviews or questionnaires that they experience such emotional changes premenstrually (69, 91, 55). Schoolgirls both receive and mete out a disproportionate amount of punishment during these days (20). Female prisoners were found to have committed a large percentage of their crimes, and to engage in most of their in-prison misconduct, during the premenstrual period (20). Medical attention and hospitalization also increase during this period, both for illness and accidents in the general female population, and for suicide attempts and acute psychiatric crises in females with pre-existing personality disorders (38).

Thus far, no adequate physiological explanation has been advanced to account for these psychological changes. It has been proposed that a drop in progesterone (a particular progestin) without a corresponding drop in estradiol (a particular estrogen) is responsible; administration of progesterone does appear to alleviate the symptoms (55). However, these behavioral changes are not always accompanied by a predictable ratio of estradiol to progesterone (2), and can even occur cyclically in conditions in which the ovaries are not functioning cyclically (before puberty, after menopause, or after removal of the ovaries (55).

Another proposed physiological explanation is that adrenal imbalance accounts for the symptoms (55), and that while this imbalance is precipitated by the progesterone decline in cycling women, it can occur from other causes in the absence of ovarian cycles. The adrenal imbalance would lead to fluid retention and weight gain, and also to behavioral changes (55). This explanation depends on the joint occurrence of both the physical and the psychological changes, whether they are causally related to each other or independent effects of the same mechanism. Unfortunately, the linkage is not consistent. In many cases, fluid retention is not associated with the symptoms, either in timing or in severity (55, 108). In one study of patients with the characteristic premenstrual behavioral changes, some individuals had higher salt and water retention and weight gain at midcycle; others actually showed a weight loss premenstrually (108). Thus, it has not been possible to explain the reported psychological components of the premenstrual syndrome by any known physiological mechanism.

At first glance, the over-all impression from the scientific literature is that the incidence of the premenstrual syndrome is fairly high. However, there are many problems with the various reports. Some have had biased samples, consisting only of persons displaying the symptoms, or only of those with regular menstrual cycles (114, 94). Moreover, different studies have measured different symptoms, making comparisons difficult; and the symptoms were often vaguely defined (114).

Many studies had no controls, no statistical analysis, could not be replicated, did not observe the same individuals over a period of time, and did not adequately define or ascertain the phases of the cycle (114, 95). Since it is much less common to publish negative findings, positive reports may be overrepresented (95). Considering all these factors, the actual incidence of the premenstrual syndrome may be lower than it appears to be.

Interestingly, reports of the incidence of the behavioral component of the syndrome differ markedly, from 0 per cent to 90 per cent of the group observed (96, 91, 108, 55). One possible explanation for such statistical variability among the studies is that the behavioral phenomenon is a highly suggestible one. In long-term studies of the same individuals, the symptoms are always reported to be highest during the first cycle observed (39). If the subjects are aware of the theory under investigation, it can lead to self-fulfilling prophecy (94). When the subjects' expectations are altered or controlled in a study, there may be no differences during the cycle (114). Self-report measures involving recall of past events are not reliably correlated with self-reports made daily (95). Moreover, tests of performance at a task do not always correlate with self-reports of mood (114). Thus, the high incidence of behavioral changes reported in a particular study may be a product of the observation method.

There is further evidence that the phenomenon, where it actually exists, has a psychological basis. It has been reported that: the syndrome is more common in more generally anxious women (112), or in neurotic women (108); that the only women who suffer significantly from the syndrome are those who were not prepared by their mothers for the first menstruation (32); that women who complain of premenstrual symptoms (i.e., do not repress their feelings) make fewer premenstrual suicide attempts than noncomplainers (38); that women not living with a man make fewer premenstrual suicide attempts (38); and that premenstrual hostility, thoughts of suicide, and suicide attempts are more likely if there is a more severe history of past medical and gynecologic disorders and of more sexual and marital problems (38).

Even if there actually is a set of premenstrual physiological factors which produces or facilitates the development of certain behaviors, the menstrual cyclicity is merely one of many regular biological rhythms. For instance, predictable fluctuations occur over a twenty-four-hour period—in both males and females—in the secretions of the adrenals and gonads, as well as in other aspects of physiology such as body temperature, blood pressure, drug sensitivity, asthmatic susceptibility, pain tolerance, sensory sensitivity, brain biochemistry and performance on psychological tests (73). Thirty-day cycles are also quite common; they have been described for plants, invertebrates, some nonprimate vertebrates, and adult human males (102). Monthly cycles in normal men have been reported for body temperature (67), weight (73), beard growth (47), pain threshold (113), and emotion (73). Quite predictable male cycles can also occur in the manifestation of catatonic or acute schizophrenia, manic-depressiveness, and epilepsy (103).

Since the onset of menstruation is so readily detected, menstrual cyclicity has always been apparent. It has thus been easy to look for correlations of physiological and behavioral phenomena. But it is equally possible that the expectation of impending menstruation, which is a negative condition in most societies, is sufficient to produce or enhance behavioral changes, particularly if the individual's life permits the luxury of behavioral disruptions. It has been pointed out that women in high-paying, responsible jobs are less likely to report the premenstrual syndrome (100), just as men in similar positions are less likely to alter their activity when afflicted with the common cold (5). Thus, the evidence for a truly physiological cause of premenstrual hostility is as shaky as the evidence for a high incidence of such behavior.

Sexual Behavior

As in the area of aggressive behavior, extrapolations have been made from the sexual behavior of subhuman primates to that of humans. Reference has been made to the early emergence of different mating patterns, the consistency of those patterns, and the dependency of the female on hormones. Let us examine each of these areas for clues to the biological contribution to the behavior.

In several primate species, young males show mounting behavior (44). Even in the first six months, rhesus males make brief, incomplete sexual reactions (rubbing, thrusting to other infants) (48). A male chimpanzee at one year can already perform a nearly complete repertoire of copulatory behaviors (57). It is important to note, however, that mounting behavior differs in young males and females only in frequency; females also show mounting behavior (8). Moreover, both sexes show the "feminine" mating posture with equal frequency.

In the adult, most of the sexual posturing is typical of the gender. However, wild-born female rhesus monkeys do show considerable amounts of mounting behavior, including the adult masculine type of foot clasp, pelvic thrusts, and apparently, occasional orgasm (85). As in rodents, dogs, and farm animals, primate females show the most frequent mounting behavior when most receptive sexually (85).

Prenatal androgens seem to have some role in shaping masculine mating behavior in the rhesus. If females are prenatally exposed to an androgen, they will show more mounting behavior as youngsters (27). If they are injected with an androgen as adults, they will show a further increase in masculine copulatory behavior, and may even ejaculate (27). Such an increase cannot be produced in normal adult females injected with an androgen (41).

It appears that learning contributes heavily to the development of the complete mating pattern, at least the masculine one. This is true even for lower mammals such as the guinea pig. Young animals perfect mounting behavior gradually, with practice, as they learn social interaction (126). If mammals are reared under socially deprived conditions (alone or in sex-segregated groups), there will frequently be some impairment of the mating performance—shorter mating episodes, poor orientation for mounting, aggression, or even complete failure to mate (48, 126). These combined deficiencies are seldom repaired.

Masculine sexual behavior is by no means completely dependent on adult androgen secretion. Castration of the male does not immediately eliminate mating (even in the rat, guinea pig, or cat), if there has been prior sexual experience (104, 84). In the female mammal, mating is more closely related to adult secretion of hormones. In most species, females are receptive to the male during a restricted period around the time of ovulation; even subhuman primates show most of their mating during this period. Female mammals will usually refuse to mate after removal of the ovaries. Replacement of the ovarian hormones will restore sexual receptivity; the exact timing requirements for estrogen and progestin administration vary among the species. In the rhesus monkey, estradiol induces receptivity, while progesterone diminishes it (86). (Testosterone, a specific androgen, also promotes sexual behavior in rhesus females after ovarian removal [86]. More will be said about testosterone and female sexuality in the discussion of women and hormones.)

Primate females are not complete slaves to their hormones. Among the most primitive primates, variation occurs in the proportion of the "heat" period during which the female will actually permit mating (41). In the rhesus, females exhibit various copulatory patterns. Mating may occur continuously at high levels throughout the cycle, continuously at low levels throughout the cycle, in one peak around ovulation, or in two peaks at ovulation and the onset of menstruation (86). The absolute levels of mating can vary a great deal, both between and within pairs. Despite preselection on the basis of good interaction, less than 50 per cent of pairs have a clear rhythm, and even then, the rhythm is not necessarily consistent in successive cycles (83). Moreover, a few females will mate long after ovariectomy (86). Clearly, there are individual differences in females, as well as in males, with incomplete dependence on hormones and an effect of past experience.

It is also clear that the female mammal is not totally passive. Some female dogs will mate readily with certain males and vigorously reject others (8). Female rhesus (86) and even female rats (10) will learn to press a bar to obtain access to a male. Rhesus sexual behavior is generally initiated by the female (48), and the number or frequency of her invitational gestures will vary with the male (86). Lever-pressing for a male will also depend on the identity of the partner (86).

There is even considerable diversity in the style of

sexual behavior among the species of subhuman primates (8). The pattern of mounting ranges from a series of mounts, to one mount with ejaculation in a few seconds, to one mount with ejaculation delayed for minutes. Some species masturbate often, others apparently not at all. Prepubertal sex play can occur. A few species show a ventral-ventral coital position.

In humans, the variability and relative freedom from gonadal hormones are greatly expanded. Androgens can apparently affect libido in adult men: if an anti-androgen is administered, libido may be depressed (70); eunuchs gain libido and potency with androgen treatment (120). But the role of experience is enormous. Even with precocious puberty, sexual behavior still tends not to appear until the appropriate age (44). If castration occurs before puberty, prior to the development of secondary sex characteristics and prior to sexual experience, there is usually no genital sexuality (118). If castration occurs after puberty, mating will often continue, to an extent dependent on the individual. Many of the men who are treated successfully with an anti-androgen for hypersexuality or sexual perversion do not revert to their former patterns when treatment is discontinued; they learn to modify their behavior (70). Impotence is not correlated with low levels of androgens, nor can it be cured with androgen therapy (120).

Female libido also seems to be partially affected by androgens. Androgen-producing tumors of the ovary or adrenal may result in excessive libido (120). Administration of testosterone can cause increased libido in normal women (118), or normal libido in frigid women (120). Removal of the adrenals, the main androgen source in women, may result in a decrease of libido (118). Ovarian hormones apparently have little role in human female sex drive (118). In contrast to subhuman

mammals, removal of a woman's ovaries does not necessarily produce any change in coital patterns (118). Administration of an estrogen may be followed either by
an increase in libido or by no change (106, 94). There
have been reports that female libido varies with the
menstrual cycle, in a faint echo of the subhuman primate pattern, with the highest frequency of mating in
midcycle, around the time of ovulation (45). But there
are also many reports that libido is highest premenstrually (94), when hormonal conditions are quite different. Progesterone reportedly decreases libido in
women (as in monkeys), and it has been used to treat
nymphomania (42). However, other studies report increases or no change of libido with progesterone (94).
It is notable in this regard that progesterone has strong
general anesthetic properties, in contrast to the androgens' stimulatory effects on metabolism (43). Hence,
hormonal effects on libido may be due to fundamental
influences on the general level of metabolic activity.

There is little factual basis for the belief that males
need sex more than do females. It is more likely that
men do not exercise so much control over sexual behavior (116). Male sexual behavior is condoned, even encouraged, whereas females are taught restraint in sexual
expression (116). Females are denied the opportunity
"to learn to be sexual" during childhood and adolescence (110). In other societies, the effects of conditioning are clear. If sex behavior in the young is controlled
in a particular society, such control is more pronounced
for the females (21). The expected female roles in initiating coitus, activity during coitus, and experience of
orgasm vary widely from culture to culture (80).

The Kinsey reports on men (59) and women (60)
found considerable sex differences in the response to
visual and narrative stimuli. Women were found to be
much less likely than men to be aroused by explicitly

sexual or isolated stimuli, such as a single picture, though there was little difference between men and women for continuous stimuli (moving pictures or literary material). However, the Kinsey reports obtained retrospective information through interviews, which can involve conscious or unconscious editing by the subject. Recent carefully controlled experiments (110) using slides, films, and stories have indicated that there is little gender difference either in the physiological reactions or in the self-ratings of sexual arousal during exposure to any of the stimuli. Although females did have a greater tendency to be shocked, this may be due to less experience with such stimuli. During the twenty-four hours following the test, there seemed to be little difference between the sexes in nonsexual emotions, sexual fantasies, desire for or incidence of coitus, coital foreplay and technique, or incidence of orgasm. In general, females were as aroused as males by the films, and even more aroused by the stories. Thus, females can react to visual and narrative stimuli to the same extent and in the same direction as males, even with little or no experience with such material. These findings have been corroborated by other reports (110). Where larger differences exist, they are probably culturally derived (32).

The choice of sexual object is another widely discussed aspect of reproductive behavior. Homosexuality, as we define it in man, is not found in subhuman primates; although they may occasionally mount or lick the genitals of a same-sex individual, they do not choose same-sex partners for intercourse (119). One must distinguish exclusive homosexuality from bisexuality and occasional homosexuality. Kinsey (59) reported that 5 per cent of American men are exclusive homosexuals and 50 per cent exclusive heterosexuals (ignoring adolescent experiences). Therefore, almost half of Kinsey's male population had sexual encounters with both sexes during their adult lives. In some cultures, homosexuality is the norm for unmarried young men, or common among married men (31). Thus, choice of sex object is not necessarily a permanent phenomenon—it may be flexible as to time and situation.

Nonetheless, for more than half of individuals, either a heterosexual or a homosexual identity and pattern of activity are firmly ingrained and persistent. It is difficult to find a biological basis for an exclusive orientation. Almost all homosexuals have normal chromosomal constitutions (107). Some evidence suggests a genetic contribution to homosexuality (22). Two different studies comparing identical twins and fraternal twins found that in 95–100 per cent of the pairs of identical twins, either both or neither one of the twins was homosexual. When both were homosexual, they were even similar in type and extent of behavior. The likelihood that common "imprint" experiences accounted for the coincidence was ruled out, because the fraternal twins pairs showed low coincidence of homosexuality or heterosexuality. It is difficult, however, to imagine the nature of a biological factor which might account for this consistency in identical twin pairs. One must presume a uniform, internal effect unrelated to the embryonic environment.

Low androgen production by the fetuses does not seem to be a likely explanation, since there is no evidence that prenatal androgens influence the choice of sex object. In the XXY syndrome, despite low fetal androgen levels, only a small minority have any problems of sex adjustment beyond a relatively weak libido (107). Females with prenatal masculinization of the genitals produced by maternal progestin treatment do not have lesbian fantasies or activities (89). Even in females with the adrenogenital syndrome who are not treated until long after birth, the incidence of homosexual fantasies has been reported as zero in a group of Soviet women (71), or moderate in an American group (89). In the American group (89), only a small percentage had had any homosexual experience, and none was exclusively lesbian. The enhanced bisexuality could be explained by the presence of more manipulable genitals, leading to habits of sexual initiation which persisted after surgical and hormonal correction. Most had heterosexual experience, and half were married.

There is also no known correlation between homosexuality and adult levels of sex hormones. There have been conflicting reports of lower (64), normal (25), and higher (15) testosterone levels in male homosexuals, as well as reports of higher (25) estradiol. Similarly, female homosexuals have been reported to have normal testosterone and estradiol levels (30), or elevated testosterone and diminished estradiol (72). Furthermore, no masculinization of female homosexuals was found for physical measures such as genitals, secondary sex characteristics, bodily proportions, or age of puberty (30). Administration of an anti-androgen to men has no effect on the direction of their sexuality, only on the magnitude (70). Administration of testosterone to females, while enhancing libido, does not change the choice of the sex object (41).

The resistance to alternation of sexual orientation is found in heterosexuality, homosexuality, and the less common fetishisms. In all but heterosexuality, these run counter to cultural expectations and social reinforcement. While their very existence negates the possibility of strict and fixed instincts for human sexual behavior, it also seems to deny the claim that role modeling and acculturation can account for every mode of expression of sexuality (63). However, there are also known examples of "one shot" conditioning, in which immediate situational factors have produced a persistent sexual attraction to, for example, muscular women, or a particular hair style (36). We do not know what determines exclusivity or predominance of sexual object when it occurs. Unsuspected environmental factors may be as influential as unknown biological factors.

Other Activities, Interests, and Goals

It has been stated that while it is very difficult to guess what an American male will be doing at the age of twenty-five, one can predict with reasonable confidence the activities of a twenty-five-year-old female (9). Her individuality is far less relevant, and the role of wife/mother is essentially a given. Is this role biologically predetermined?

In several rodent species, both sexes engage in parental behavior, and the sex difference is quantitative rather than qualitative (127). In subhuman primates, attention to infants is almost exclusively a female activity. Neither subadult nor adult male langurs or baboons show much interest in infants, whereas female juveniles will spend much of their time with adult females, participating in infant care (35, 28). But such behavior is not automatic in females. Female rhesus monkeys raised in isolation from mothers or peers are either indifferent or abusive to their offspring, though they may eventually allow a persistent infant to nurse (48). In the gibbon, chimpanzee, and gorilla, naïve females can be frightened by the appearance of their own infants (50). Maternal behavior, even infant carrying, must be learned. First-time mothers are normally not very good mothers, and frequently reject or even attack their infants. Although this deficiency may be exaggerated in captivity, it points to the necessity of learning and observation for successful motherhood (50). As in many other types of behavior, habitat can be influential.

Within the same species of monkey, grassland animals show a stronger maternal-infant bond than do forest groups (35).

Differences between the sexes become apparent quite early in humans (111). At the age of three, there are subtle differences in the style and quality of doll play. Boys begin to specialize in vigorous romping and large muscle activity while girls follow less active pursuits. Toy choices differ. This divergence is reflected in adult occupational choices. How autonomous is the development of the divergence?

Girls with prenatal masculinization of the genitals (89, 29) have activities and interests more common to boys, and are often considered typical tomboys. Like prenatally masculinized female rhesus monkeys (41), they engage more in rough outdoor play. They are also not particularly concerned with grooming, or interested in feminine clothing and paraphernalia. They are indifferent, though not hostile, to the future likelihood of being wives/mothers. Yet these latter characteristics would follow naturally from their social environment, which is affected by their tendency to rough outdoor play. Such girls would have much less contact with other girls, and less exposure to information about "feminine" activities. Interest in feminine (more vulnerable) clothing or grooming would be a liability to their active, outdoor pursuits. They would also be likely to incorporate the values of their male associates, with an emphasis on future occupations outside the home. Nonetheless, they do eventually marry and have children—even those whose excess androgen production continued well beyond birth (89).

The opposite effect on activity has been reported in boys whose diabetic mothers were treated during pregnancy with an estrogen to prevent miscarriage (125). These individuals show diminution of athletic co-ordination, assertiveness, and masculine interests. Since male children of untreated diabetic mothers did not show similar decreases in assertiveness, the maternal illness cannot have been the cause. It is not clear whether an estrogen could have such a direct effect; it is possible that an estrogen would lead to a decrease in androgen secretion, and a consequent deficiency in masculinization. In most cases, the genitals of the boys appeared normal, suggesting that any androgen decrease was either slight, or occurred after genital differentiation. No information is available about the timing of the maternal estrogen therapy.

Thus, differences in activity and energy expenditure may differ somewhat in relation to fetal hormonal exposure. Subsequent cultural input is also extremely important for the development of sex differences. Surveys of parents have demonstrated quite different attitudes and treatment for the two sexes, in reactions to the children, methods of rearing, and importance of goals (11). The emphasis was placed on female development and maintenance of close interpersonal relationships, and on male competition and achievement. Girls were encouraged to talk about their troubles; boys were expected to control their feelings and expression of emotion. Quite early behavioral sex typing by parents occurs in personality attributes, intellectual performance, and occupational choices (111).

When female college undergraduates reminisced about their childhoods (85), they recalled many instances of "feminine" training. They were allowed fewer opportunities for independent action (such as playing away from home, choosing the time to come home, picking their own activities, going places alone). Moreover, even these freedoms came at a later age than for their brothers. They had less privacy in their personal affairs, even at an older age, than male siblings.

The filial and kinship obligations were more exacting for interpersonal contacts, infant care, and household chores. They also received financial support in situations in which their brothers were expected to be self-supporting. In sum, there was much less opportunity for the development of independence and self-assertion.

This sort of training may well be necessary. When three-year-old children are asked to pick toys, they are not aware of sex-appropriateness (65). Working-class children adopt traditional behavior patterns earlier, illustrating the cultural influence (65). In one study of middle-class girls between six and nine years old, most preferred masculine games, objects, and activities (16). The female undergraduates mentioned above (65) recalled many instances in which their "masculine" behavior was heavily discouraged, while "feminine" behavior was censured in brothers or male contemporaries. Their own preference for soldiers, tree-climbing, football, tools, and chemistry sets was contrasted with the fact that some of the boys liked dolls. They were criticized for getting dirty, whereas the boys were teased for being neat. One even recalled being expected to cry at a funeral while her brother simultaneously tried not to.

The cultural variation in attitudes toward childbearing (dangerous and painful vs. simple and joyful; interesting, matter-of-fact, or shameful) attests to the modifiability of this behavior in females (80). Cross-generational and cross-cultural comparisons of female occupations also illustrate the need for thorough training if women are to become exclusively wives and mothers. In the 1930s, the proportion of American women in the ranks of professional and semiprofessional workers, or holding higher educational degrees, was substantially greater than at present (26). Although females represent only 6 per cent of the

M.D.s in the United States, the corresponding percentages are 16 per cent in the United Kingdom and 75 per cent in the U.S.S.R. (26). Thirty-five per cent of Russian engineers are women, whereas only 3 per cent of ninth-grade American females are even considering science or engineering careers (9). In the Tchambuli of New Guinea, the females are the strong, practical, managerial class, while the males are idle, spoiled, emotionally dependent, and engage in shopping and gossip (80).

Female "biological rhythms" associated with menstruation or pregnancy do not necessarily influence the occupational options, or otherwise interfere with the pattern of participation in the economy. In some cultures, both sexes work at essentially the same tasks and in the same pattern. In other cultures, the tasks are different, but the pattern of working is the same. In still others, it is the males who work episodically, while the females work steadily (80). Moreover, in the United States, it appears that females do not have a higher rate of absenteeism than males and, in fact, lose fewer work days to illness (26).

Intelligence and Mental Behavior

It is generally agreed that adult males and females do not differ in general intelligence but rather in specific skills (19). Females are considered to have greater verbal fluency, and males to excel in visual-spatial ability (18). There are also reports of female superiority in tasks requiring only recall, speed, and accuracy of performance (i.e., not higher thought processes), and further reports of male superiority in tasks of reasoning, restructuring, and problem solving (17). However, there is very extensive overlap among individuals in the two sexual categories; the reported differences result only when the internal diversity of the two groups is eliminated by averaging procedures (76, 53).

Although there are reports that the verbal and visual-spatial differences appear during childhood (53, 18), a recent exhaustive review of the entire literature (77) concludes that they do not really manifest themselves until later, around the time of puberty. Since the matter is equivocal, let us assume that they do appear early, and consider the possible biological influences.

Prenatal exposure to androgens might have a direct effect on neural tissue, producing functionally different brains in the two sexes. The left side of the brain controls language function, whereas the right side of the brain is responsible for spatial and nonverbal functions. The left side is normally dominant in both sexes. It has been proposed that this dominance is more complete in females, accounting for female language superiority and male visual-spatial superiority (18). Several types of evidence are cited for this conclusion. Examination of brain tissue in four-year-old children indicated greater development of some areas of the left side in females, and of the right side in males (18). In five-year-olds, females were found to be more accurate in discriminating words, which are processed by the left side, whereas males were more accurate in discriminating nonverbal noises and animal sounds, which are processed by the right side (18). Although the left side is dominant over the right side in adults, the opposite is true in children until about the age of two, when a shift occurs as linguistic skills are acquired. This transition apparently occurs later in males (18). This may account in part for their greater prevalence of general language disorders, noted above. It should be mentioned that the greater dominance of the left side in female brains is not true of all abilities; from three to eleven years of age, girls perform better than boys in drawing with the left hand (18).

If there are biologically based mental differences in childhood, they would presumably be the product of prenatal androgen influence. One would then expect that females masculinized embryonically, either through exposure to progestins or through the adrenogenital syndrome, would show a diminution of verbal ability and an increase in visual-spatial skills in comparison to the average female. They should perform more like the average male. Similarly, males with the same prenatal exposure should show below-average verbal skills and above-average visual-spatial skills when compared to other males. Unfortunately the several studies of intelligence of such children indicated an increase in general IQ, but differential abilities were not measured (6, 71).

A recent report (6) has investigated this phenomenon in adrenogenital boys and girls, comparing the patients to their parents and siblings as a control for socioeconomic status and rearing practices. However, this control group may constitute a particularly biased sample. Since the adrenogenital syndrome is produced by the presence of two recessive genes, each parent and two thirds of the siblings would carry one gene for the condition; thus, they too might have somewhat elevated androgen levels. This may explain why parents and siblings also had quite high general IQs, and why no significant differences in differential abilities were found among these groups. Though nonsignificant, some of the trends in the data were in the direction of changes expected for prenatal androgen exposure: the adrenogenital males scored the highest of all groups on performance tests; and the adrenogenital females showed no difference between verbal and performance measures. Some expected normal differences were also observed: adrenogenital females were better on verbal measures than were adrenogenital males; and female siblings' verbal measures were better than their own performance measures. But there were also some quite unexpected findings: fathers were the highest scorers on verbal measures, whereas mothers were the lowest; male siblings were the lowest on perceptual measures, and even had perceptual scores that were lower than their own verbal scores.

Thus, the evidence is inconclusive for the existence of mental differences in female and male children, and on possible causes of differences. In adolescence, qualitative mental sex differences are more readily identifiable, and persist in adulthood (77). What is the possible role of hormones in this change?

For males with an extra X chromosome (XXY) and lower levels of adult androgen production, there are reports of a tendency to be less analytic and more global in the approach to problems on intelligence tests (121). This might be construed as feminization (or inadequate masculinization) of their mental processes. However, they also show impairment of verbalization ability, which would be counter to prediction. It is likely that their more passive natures, or some direct disruptive effect of an entire extra chromosome, accounts for any mental impairment.

Females with only one X chromosome (XO) have nonfunctional ovaries. One might expect that the absence of estrogens would render their mental performance more similar to that of the average male. However, this is not the case; their performance is changed in the opposite direction. Although verbal ability is unaltered, there is actually a deficiency in perceptual organization and performance (121). Like XXY males, either their greater passivity or the impact of a major chromosomal abnormality (deficit of an entire chromosome) might be instrumental.

There is very little evidence for the direct contribution of adult androgen levels to the sex differences in mental performance. There has been a report that administration of testosterone alleviates fatigue, and facilitates the focusing of attention in the performance of a repetitive task (62). The same authors also found that a high level of performance on repetitive tasks correlated positively with androgen production and utilization, and with indications of androgen influence such as development of the chest, biceps, and pubic hair (61). It is curious that testosterone should enhance a skill which is usually cited as characteristic of female mental ability, and as detrimental to the male forte, problem solving. The authors attempt to resolve the dilemma by contending that this automatization ability is a prerequisite for the development of complex psychological processes.

It could be that over-all average differences in male-female mental performance are attributable to fluctuations in female performance with hormonal changes during the menstrual cycle. Even if female performance on a given measure is the same as male performance at most times, random testing would include enough times when it is different to produce a general decrease in female scores. There have been many studies of female mental functioning or motor performance during the menstrual cycle. Some studies have reported premenstrual decreases in correct time estimation, ability to discriminate separate flashes of light, muscular efficiency, and tests of either general intelligence or special knowledge (20, 115, 74). In other studies, however, no differences have been detected in simple reaction time, ability to recognize sensory stimuli, manual dexterity, industrial production and performance, athletic performance, and tests of general intelligence or special knowledge (55, 115, 51, 141). Moreover, some of the tests which did detect differences have been criticized for lack of controls, lack of statistics, and lack of knowledge of the individual's phase of the cycle (114). In sum, the magnitude of fluctuation detectable during the menstrual cycle seems too small to account for the over-all differences obtained in postpubertal male and female mental performances.

Adolescence is a time when special emphasis is placed on sex-typed behavior. It is plausible that the emerging gap in male-female mental abilities reflects a self-fulfilling prophecy, with societal expectations producing the expected phenomena. There is extensive evidence of a strong influence from rearing practices. In a test situation, parents who were requested to encourage preschoolers in problem solving were more likely to reject inadequate solutions, prohibit diversionary play, and maintain a standard of achievement for males (11). In many tests, female deficiency in performance may be due to lack of familiarity or experience with the activity, or the context of the problem (19). When a problem requiring abstract reasoning and mathematics is reworded to deal with cooking, female performance can be substantially improved (9). The sex of the investigator can also affect the results of a test (34).

Maccoby (76) has made an eloquent case for the influence of sex-typed personality traits, stating that the fostering of dependency and conformity in females interferes with their ability to restructure in problem solving, and that the males' lesser attention to all of the stimuli reduces their recognition or recall of details. Rare cultures in which women are not treated as dependent, such as the Canadian Eskimo (19), do not show typical male superiority in field-dependence tests, which measure the ability to respond to one aspect of a stimulus without being distracted by the background.

Since many sex differences are not apparent in early childhood, it is difficult to assume that they are innate. Moreover, some differences emerge before puberty, again undercutting a physiological or hormonal explanation. It is thus hard to deny some influence of acculturation. Fundamental expectations of performance shape the child's behavior, and these vary along sex lines. In school, for example, where female success is acceptable, females get better grades, even in subjects in which boys score higher on standard achievement tests (76). But after school, males succeed far more than females in almost every aspect of intellectual activity where comparisons can be drawn. Gifted females are far less likely to realize their potential (76). The effects of societal expectations can be quite subtle. Even other females expect less of females. In a test in which ratings were given for professional articles from various fields, both men and women gave lower ratings for identical material if there was a female name for author—even if the field was a "feminine" one such as dietetics or elementary education (9).

Conclusion

Today, virtually no one would contend that either "nature" (biology) or "nurture" (culture) alone accounts for personality and behavior. This sterile controversy is fortunately passing out of vogue, and individual human development is viewed as a perpetual interaction of biological and social forces. But there continues to be considerable discussion about the relative importance of each influence. Since the evidence is essentially inconclusive, the generalizations are largely a matter of personal interpretation. Thus far, the thorough reviews

(34, 22, 53) have emphasized the biological limitations on the individual. The present chapter considers the same information and arrives at another point of view.

The actual physical differences between the sexes (besides the obvious ones of internal and external genitals) can be summarized easily. Adult hormonal secretion in the male is continuous, and consists primarily of androgens. In the female, hormonal secretion is cyclic, with separate phases of estrogen and progestin predominance. Males and females differ in shape, size, muscularity, endurance in physical exertion, and (possibly) metabolic rate. These differences can be minimized when both sexes engage in the same activities, but are not entirely eliminated. Slight sex differences exist in sensitivity to touch, but the evidence is contradictory for sight, sound, taste, and smell. Females mature faster than males; this discrepancy is probably largely independent of cultural influence. Males seem to be more susceptible to physical disorders. Of course, typical male activities often exacerbate this tendency, and social attitudes may contribute to the development or recognition of particular illnesses.

Behavioral differences between the sexes are apparent at birth. Males are more irritable, show grosser body movements, and are less responsive to touch. Sex differences in treatment also begin at birth, and separation of the relative biological and social contributions is thus complicated from the outset.

Aggression is slightly more common in males, both before and after puberty. There is inadequate evidence on the effects of prenatal androgens, but it is clear that parental tolerance of aggressiveness differs for the sexes. The role of adult androgen secretion in aggression is also unclear. In some females, it is possible that hostility increases premenstrually, although the responsible physiological factors have not been defined. Psychological influences on this phenomenon are quite pronounced. Other cycles in men and women receive less attention because they lack such a visible cue.

Adult androgen levels may contribute to libido, but so can experience and attitude. Other hormones seem to have little effect. Cultural factors influence the types of stimuli which cause arousal, and the choice of sex object. The evidence for homosexual predisposition due to either prenatal or postpubertal hormonal levels is scanty and inconclusive.

Choices of activities and goals are quite sex-typed. Although girls exposed prenatally to androgens seem to have more masculine interests, this could be because their higher energy level causes them to associate more with boys. While there are certain similarities in female occupations across many cultures, there are so many qualitative and quantitative exceptions that a more likely explanation is the institutionalization of differences which were originally necessary to provide for pregnancy and child care.

Since there is disagreement about the actual existence of qualitative sex differences in intelligence prior to puberty, and only the slightest evidence of how these might be produced biologically, the point remains moot. The demonstrable mental differences in adolescents and adults have not yet been clearly linked to any biological factors. In any case, strong cultural influences on postpubertal intellectual performance can be discerned.

Taken together, the information on sex differences in behavior suggests that three statements might summarize the responsible factors: first is the familiar "You are what you eat," to which could be added, "You are what you secrete," and "You are whom you meet."

As an expedient for purposes of discussion, the preceding summary treated sex differences as real and large, essentially polar opposites. This position is quite artificial. Most characteristics are found in both sexes; the more common difference is in the positive or negative value attached to a characteristic, depending on who has it. It is absurd to state that *the* female does something. At best, it can be said that more females than males do a particular thing, or that females are more likely to do one thing than another. An individual is not more or less masculine, or more or less feminine, but rather more or less aggressive, sexual, nurturant, ambitious, verbal, spatial, and so on. If certain females are more "masculine" in aggressiveness or intelligence than the average male, and yet have normal female genitals and menstrual cycles, then one must either postulate that their prenatal masculinization did not occur until a later stage of brain development, or simply admit that there is enormous overlap between the sexes. The converse applies for theories of insufficient masculinization of males who are structurally normal but behaviorally more like the average female. Money and Ehrhardt (89) have suggested that children are not restricted to learning only one set of gender-appropriate behavior, but that they actually learn two separate systems: what they should do and be, and what the other sex should do and be. Indeed, it has been observed that incongruous behavior, typical of the opposite sex, may be released under certain conditions of mental deterioration such as senility or epilepsy in a particular brain region (88).

In view of the similarities in behavior between males and females, and the differences within each sex, gender is too broad a category for predicting an individual's characteristics. If any sort of biological determinism exists, it is responsible for much more subtle variations. The scientifically (and ethically) ideal approach would be to determine each individual's potential, regardless of gender or other group affiliation, and then encourage development of positive abilities and compensation for deficiencies. As Bem and Bem (9) have pointed out, a person's primary activity should be based on his or her unique interests, rather than on the grounds of belonging to a group which has some average characteristic.

Certain societies do have this sort of flexibility, allowing males to assume female roles and activities (81). In contemporary industrialized societies, the artificial distinctions which do exist between the sexes may be holdovers from human prehistoric experience. There is little need now for a division of labor based upon physical strength or endurance. There is also little need to ensure that all occupational slots are filled, by "tracking" children at an early age. Indeed, early tracking may even lessen the efficiency of the economy, because of poor performance in the many instances of bad fit. It has the further disadvantage of limiting individual and societal flexibility and adaptability to changing needs. And finally, there is certainly precious little current need to maintain sexual distinctiveness so as to maximize human fertility rates.

In summary, while it need not and cannot be argued that the individual human being is a biological *tabula rasa* at birth, the slate of *a priori* assumptions concerning social-biological characteristics should be blank.

References

1. Abramovich, D. R., and P. Rowe, 1973. "Foetal plasma testosterone levels at mid-pregnancy and at term: relationship to foetal sex." *J. Endo*. 56, 621–22.

2. Adamopoulos, D. A., J. A. Loraine, S. F. Lunn, A. J. Coppen, and R. J. Daly, 1972. "Endocrine profiles in premenstrual tension." *Clin. Endo*. 1, 283–92.

3. Andersen, H., 1966. "The influence of hormones on

human development." Pp. 184–221 in Falkner, F. (ed.), *Human Development*. Philadelphia: Saunders.

4. Archer, J., 1973. "Sex differences in emotional behaviour: a reply to Gray and Buffery." *Acta. Psychol.* 35, 415–29.

5. Aronson, L. A., 1973. In discussion of Ramey, E. R., "Sex hormones and executive ability." *Ann. N.Y. Acad. Sci.* 208, 237–54.

6. Baker, S. W., and A. A. Ehrhardt, 1974. "Prenatal androgen, intelligence and cognitive sex differences." Pp. 53–76 in Friedman, R. C. (ed.), *Sex Differences in Behavior*. New York: Wiley.

7. Barry, H., III, M. K. Bacon, and I. L. Child, 1957. "A cross-cultural survey of some sex differences in socialization." *J. Abn. Soc. Psychol.* 55, 327–32.

8. Beach, F. A., 1965. "Retrospect and prospect." Pp. 535–69 in Beach, F. A. (ed.), (Conference on) *Sex and Behavior*. New York: Wiley.

9. Bem, S. L., and D. J. Bem, 1970. "Case study of a nonconscious ideology: training the woman to know her place." Pp. 89–99 in Bem, D. J., *Beliefs, Attitudes and Human Affairs*. Belmont, California: Brooks/Cole.

10. Bermant, G., 1961. "Response latencies of female rats during sexual intercourse." *Science* 133, 1771–73.

11. Block, J. H., 1973. "Conceptions of sex role: some cross-cultural and longitudinal perspectives." *Amer. Psychol.* 28, 512–26.

12. Bodmer, W. F., 1971. Letter to the London *Times*, December 23.

13. Boon, D. A., R. E. Keenan, W. R. Slaunwhite, Jr., and T. Aceto, Jr., 1972. "Conjugated and unconjugated plasma androgens in normal children." *Pediat. Res.* 6, 111–18.

14. Brasel, J. A., 1968. "Oxygen consumption and growth." Pp. 474–93 in Cheek, D. B. (ed.), *Human Growth*. Philadelphia: Lea and Febiger.

15. Brodie, H. K. H., N. Gartrell, C. Doering, and T. Rhue, 1974. "Plasma testosterone levels in heterosexual and homosexual men." *Amer. J. Psychiat.* 131, 82–83.

16. Brown, D. G., 1958. "Sex-role development in a changing culture." *Psychol. Bull.* 55, 232–42.

17. Broverman, D. M., E. L. Klaiber, Y. Kobayashi, and W. Vogel, 1968. "Roles of activation and inhibition in sex differences in cognitive abilities." *Psychol. Rev.* 75, 23–50.

18. Buffery, A. W. H., and J. A. Gray, 1972. "Sex differences in the development of spatial and linguistic skills." Pp. 123–57 in Ounsted, C., and D. C. Taylor (eds.), *Gender Differences: Their Ontogeny and Significance.* Baltimore: Williams and Wilkins.

19. Coates, S., 1974. "Sex differences in field independence among pre-school children." Pp. 259–74 in Friedman, R. C. (ed.), *Sex Differences in Behavior.* New York: Wiley.

20. Dalton, K., 1964. *The Premenstrual Syndrome.* Springfield, Illinois: Thomas.

21. D'Andrade, R. G., 1966. "Sex differences and cultural institutions." Pp. 174–204 in Maccoby, E. E. (ed.), *The Development of Sex Differences.* Stanford: Stanford University Press.

22. Diamond, M., 1965. "A critical evaluation of the ontogeny of human sexual behavior." *Quart. Rev. Biol.* 40, 147–75.

23. Diamond, M., A. L. Diamond, and M. Mast, 1972. "Visual sensitivity and sexual arousal levels during the menstrual cycle." *J. Nerv. Ment. Dis.* 155, 170–76.

24. Doering, C. H., H. K. H. Brodie, H. Kraemer, H. Becker, and D. A. Hamburg, 1974. "Plasma testosterone levels and psychologic measures in men over a 2-month period." Pp. 413–31 in Friedman, R. C. (ed.), *Sex Differences in Behavior.* New York: Wiley.

25. Doerr, P., G. Kockott, H. J. Vogt, K. M. Pirke, and F. Dittmar, 1973. "Plasma testosterone, estradiol and semen analysis in male homosexuals." *Arch. Gen. Psychiat.* 29, 829–33.

26. Dornbusch, S. M., 1966. "Afterword." Pp. 205–19 in Maccoby, E. E. (ed.), *The Development of Sex Differences.* Stanford: Stanford University Press.

27. Eaton, G. G., R. W. Goy, and C. H. Phoenix, 1973. "Effects of testosterone treatment in adulthood on sexual behavior of female pseudohermaphrodite rhesus monkeys." *Nature New Biology* 242, 119–20.

28. Ehrhardt, A. A., 1973. "Maternalism in fetal hormonal

and related syndromes." Pp. 99–115 in Zubin, J., and J. Money (eds.), *Contemporary Sexual Behavior: Critical Issues in the 1970s.* Baltimore: The Johns Hopkins University Press.

29. Ehrhardt, A. A., and S. W. Baker, 1974. "Fetal androgens, human central nervous system differentiation, and (behavior) sex differences." Pp. 33–51 in Friedman, R. C. (ed.), *Sex Differences in Behavior.* New York: Wiley.

30. Eisinger, A. J., R. G. Huntsman, and J. Lord, 1972. "Female homosexuality." *Nature* 238, 106.

31. Ford, C. S., and F. A. Beach, 1951. *Patterns of Sexual Behavior.* New York: Harper & Row.

32. Gadpaille, W. J., 1973. "Innate masculine-feminine differences." *Med. Asp. Hum. Sexuality* 7, 141–57.

33. Garai, J. E., 1970. "Sex differences in mental health." *Gen. Psychol. Monogr.* 81, 123–42.

34. Garai, J. E., and A. Scheinfeld, 1968. "Sex differences in mental and behavioral traits." *Gen. Psychol. Monogr.* 77, 169–299.

35. Gartlan, J. S., and C. K. Brain, 1968. "Ecology and social variability in *Cercopithecus aethiops* and *C. mitis.*" Pp. 253–92 in Jay, P. C. (ed.), *Primates. Studies in Adaptation and Variability.* New York: Holt, Rinehart & Winston.

36. Gebhard, P. H., 1965. Situational factors affecting human sexual behavior. Pp. 483–95 in Beach, F. A. (ed.), (Conference on) *Sex and Behavior.* New York: Wiley.

37. Gewirtz, H. B., and J. L. Gewirtz, 1968. "Visiting and caretaking patterns for kibbutz infants: age and sex trends." *Amer. J. Orthopsychiat.* 38, 427–43.

38. Glass, G. S., G. R. Heninger, M. Lansky, and K. Talan, 1971. "Psychiatric emergency related to the menstrual cycle." *Amer. J. Psychiat.* 128, 705–11.

39. Goldzieher, J. W., L. E. Moses, E. Averkin, C. Scheel, and B. Z. Taber, 1971. "Nervousness and depression attributed to oral contraceptives: a double-blind, placebo-controlled study." *Amer. J. Obstet. Gynecol.* 111, 1013–20.

40. Goy, R. W., 1968. "Organizing effects of androgen on the behaviour of rhesus monkeys." Pp. 12–31 in

Michael, R. P. (ed.), *Endocrinology and Human Behaviour*. New York: Oxford University Press.

41. Goy, R. W., and J. A. Resko, 1972. "Gonadal hormones and behavior of normal and pseudohermaphroditic nonhuman female primates." *Rec. Progr. Horm. Res.* 28, 707–33.

42. Greenblatt, R. B., 1972. Remark in discussion of "Hormones and Behavior" Session. *Rec. Progr. Horm. Res.* 28, 760–61.

43. Hamburg, D. A., 1963. "Effects of progesterone on behavior." *Res. Publ. Ass. Nerv. Ment. Dis.* 43, 251–65.

44. Hamburg, D. A., and D. T. Lunde, 1966. "Sex hormones in the development of sex differences in human behavior." Pp. 1–24 in Maccoby, E. E. (ed.), *The Development of Sex Differences*. Stanford: Stanford University Press.

45. Hamburg, D. A., R. H. Moos, and I. D. Yalom, 1968. "Studies of distress in the menstrual cycle and the postpartum period." Pp. 94–116 in Michael, R. P. (ed.), *Endocrinology and Human Behaviour*. New York: Oxford University Press.

46. Hampson, J. L., 1965. "Determinants of psychosexual orientation." Pp. 108–132 in Beach, F. A. (ed.), (Conference on) *Sex and Behavior*. New York: Wiley.

47. Harkness, R. A., 1974. "Variations in testosterone excretion by man." Pp. 469–78 in Ferin, M., F. Halberg, R. M. Richart, and R. L. Vande Wiele (eds.), *Biorhythms and Human Reproduction*. New York: Wiley.

48. Harlow, H. F., 1965. "Sexual behavior in the rhesus monkey." Pp. 234–65 in Beach, F. A. (ed.), (Conference on) *Sex and Behavior*. New York: Wiley.

49. Harlow, H. F., and M. K. Harlow, 1965. "The effect of rearing conditions on behavior." Pp. 161–75 in Money, J. (ed.), *Sex Research: New Developments*. New York: Holt, Rinehart & Winston.

50. Hediger, H., 1965. "Environmental factors influencing the reproduction of zoo animals." Pp. 319–54 in Beach, F. A. (ed.), (Conference on) *Sex and Behavior*. New York: Wiley.

51. Henkin, R. I., 1974. "Sensory changes during the

menstrual cycle." Pp. 277–85 in Ferin, M., F. Halberg, R. M. Richart, and R. L. Vande Wiele (eds.), *Biorhythms and Human Reproduction.* New York: Wiley.

52. Hunt, E. E., Jr., 1966. "The developmental genetics of man." Pp. 76–122 in Falkner, F. (ed.), *Human Development.* Philadelphia: Saunders.

53. Hutt, C., 1972. *Males and Females.* Baltimore: Penguin.

54. Hutt, C., 1972. "Neuroendocrinological, behavioural, and intellectual aspects of sexual differentiation in human development." Pp. 73–121 in Ounsted, C., and D. C. Taylor (eds.), *Gender Differences: Their Ontogeny and Significance.* Baltimore: Williams and Wilkins.

55. Janowsky, D. S., R. Gorney, and A. J. Mandell, 1967. "The menstrual cycle. Psychiatric and ovarian-adrenocortical hormone correlates: case study and literature review." *Arch. Gen. Psychiat.* 17, 459–69.

56. Jay, P. C., 1968. "Comments." Pp. 173–79 in Jay, P. C. (ed.), *Primates. Studies in Adaptation and Variability.* New York: Holt, Rinehart & Winston.

57. Jensen, G. D., 1973. "Human sexual behavior in primate perspective." Pp. 17–31 in Zubin, J., and J. Money (eds.), *Contemporary Sexual Behavior: Critical Issues in the 1970s.* Baltimore: The Johns Hopkins University Press.

58. Joslyn, W. D., 1973. "Androgen-induced social dominance in infant female rhesus monkeys." *J. Child Psychol. Psychiat.* 14, 137–45.

59. Kinsey, A. C., W. B. Pomeroy, and C. E. Martin, 1948. *Sexual behavior in the human male.* Philadelphia: Saunders.

60. Kinsey, A. C., W. B. Pomeroy, C. E. Martin, and P. H. Gebhard, 1953. *Sexual Behavior in the Human Female.* Philadelphia: Saunders.

61. Klaiber, E. L., D. M. Broverman, W. Vogel, and E. J. Mackenberg, 1974. "Rhythms in cognitive functioning and EEG indices in males." Pp. 481–93 in Ferin, M., F. Halberg, R. M. Richart, and R. L. Vande Wiele (eds.), *Biorhythms and Human Reproduction.* New York: Wiley.

62. Klaiber, E. L., D. M. Broverman, W. Vogel, G. E.

Abraham, and F. L. Cone, 1971. Effects of infused testosterone on mental performance and serum LH. *J. Clin. End. Metab.* 32, 341–49.

63. Kohlberg, L., 1966. "A cognitive-developmental analysis of children's sex-role concepts and attitudes." Pp. 82–173 in Maccoby, E. E. (ed.), *The Development of Sex Differences.* Stanford: Stanford University Press.

64. Kolodny, R. C., W. H. Masters, J. Hendryx, and G. Toro, 1971. "Plasma testosterone and semen analysis in male homosexuals." *New Engl. J. Med.* 285, 1170–74.

65. Komarovsky, M., 1964. "Learning the feminine role." Pp. 213–23 in Schur, E. M. (ed.), *The Family and the Sexual Revolution.* Bloomington: Indiana University Press.

66. Korner, A. F., 1974. "Methodological considerations in studying sex differences in the behavioral functioning of newborns." Pp. 197–208 in Friedman, R. C. (ed.), *Sex Differences in Behavior.* New York: Wiley.

67. Kuhl, J. F. W., J. K. Lee, F. Halberg, E. Haus, R. Günther, and E. Knapp, 1974. "Circadian and lower frequency rhythms in male grip strength and baby weight." Pp. 529–48 in Ferin, M., F. Halberg, R. M. Richart, and R. L. Vande Wiele (eds.), *Biorhythms and Human Reproduction.* New York: Wiley.

68. Kummer, H., 1968. "Two variations in the social organization of baboons." Pp. 293–312 in Jay, P. C. (ed.), *Primates. Studies in Adaptation and Variability.* New York: Holt, Rinehart & Winston.

69. Kutner, S. J., and W. L. Brown, 1972. "Types of oral contraceptives, depression, and premenstrual symptoms." *J. Nerv. Ment. Dis.* 155, 153–62.

70. Laschet, U., 1973. "Antiandrogen in the treatment of sex offenders: mode of action and therapeutic outcome." Pp. 311–19 in Zubin, J., and J. Money (eds.), *Contemporary Sexual Behavior: Critical Issues in the 1970s.* Baltimore: The Johns Hopkins University Press.

71. Lev-ran, A., 1974. "Sexuality and educational levels of women with the late-treated adrenogenital syndrome." *Arch. Sex Behav.* 3, 27–32.

72. Loraine, J. A., A. A. A. Ismail, D. A. Adamopoulos, and G. A. Dove, 1970. "Endocrine function in male and female homosexuals." *Brit. Med. J.* 4, 406–8.

73. Luce, G. G., 1971. *Biological Rhythms in Human and Animal Physiology.* New York: Dover.

74. Lunde, D. T., and D. A. Hamburg, 1972. "Techniques for assessing the effects of sex hormones on affect, arousal, and aggression in humans." *Rec. Progr. Horm. Res.* 28, 627–63.

75. Lyon, M. F., 1961. "Gene action in the X-chromosome of the mouse (*Mus musculus* L.)." *Nature* 190, 372–73.

76. Maccoby, E. E., 1966. "Sex differences in intellectual functioning." Pp. 25–55 in Maccoby, E. E. (ed.), *The Development of Sex Differences.* Stanford: Stanford University Press.

77. Maccoby, E. E., and C. N. Jacklin, 1974. *The Psychology of Sex Differences.* Stanford: Stanford University Press.

78. Madigan, F. C., 1957. "Are sex mortality differentials biologically caused?" *Milbank Memor. Fund Quart.* 35, 202–23.

79. Marshall, W. A., 1970. "Sex differences at puberty." *J. Biosoc. Sci., Suppl.* 2, 31–41.

80. Mead, M., 1949. *Male and Female.* New York: Morrow.

81. Mensh, I., 1972. "Personal and social environmental influences in the development of gender identity." Pp. 41–55 in Ounsted, C., and D. C. Taylor (eds.), *Gender Differences: Their Ontogeny and Significance.* Baltimore: Williams and Wilkins.

82. Meyer-Bahlburg, H. F. L., 1974. "Aggression, androgens, and the XYY syndrome." Pp. 433–53 in Friedman, R. C. (ed.), *Sex Differences in Behavior.* New York: Wiley.

83. Michael, R. P., 1968. "Gonadal hormones and the control of primate behaviour." Pp. 69–93 in Michael, R. P. (ed.), *Endocrinology and Human Behaviour.* New York: Oxford University Press.

84. Michael, R. P., 1972. "Determinants of primate reproductive behavior." *Acta. Endo. Suppl.* 166, 322–63.

85. Michael, R. P., 1974. "The bisexual behavior of female rhesus monkeys." Pp. 399–412 in Friedman,

R. C. (ed.), *Sex Differences in Behavior*. New York: Wiley.

86. Michael, R. P., D. Zumpe, E. B. Keverne, and R. W. Bonsall, 1972. "Neuroendocrine factors in the control of primate behavior." *Rec. Prog. Horm. Res.* 28, 665–706.

87. Mischel, W., 1966. "A social-learning view of sex differences in behavior." Pp. 56–81 in Maccoby, E. E. (ed.), *The Development of Sex Differences*. Stanford: Stanford University Press.

88. Money, J., 1973. "Sexology: behavioral, cultural, hormonal, neurological, genetic, etc." *J. Sex Res.* 9, 3–10.

89. Money, J., and A. A. Ehrhardt, 1972. *Man & Woman, Boy & Girl.* Baltimore: The Johns Hopkins University Press.

90. Moss, H. A., 1974. "Early sex differences and mother-infant interaction." Pp. 149–63 in Friedman, R. C. (ed.), *Sex Differences in Behavior*. New York: Wiley.

91. Moss, R. H., B. S. Kopell, F. T. Melges, I. D. Yalom, D. T. Lunde, R. B. Clayton, and D. A. Hamburg, 1969. "Fluctuations in symptoms and moods during the menstrual cycle." *J. Psychosom. Res.* 13, 37–44.

92. Moyer, K. E., 1974. "Sex differences in aggression." Pp. 335–72 in Friedman, R. C. (ed.), *Sex Differences in Behavior*. New York: Wiley.

93. Mukherjee, B. B., and R. G. Milet, 1972. "Nonrandom X-chromosome inactivation—an artifact of cell selection." *Proc. Nat. Acad. Sci.* 69, 37–39.

94. O'Connor, J. F., E. M. Shelley, and L. O. Stern, 1974. "Behavioral rhythms related to the menstrual cycle." Pp. 309–24 in Ferin, M., F. Halberg, R. M. Richart, and R. L. Vande Wiele (eds.), *Biorhythms and Human Reproduction*. New York: Wiley.

95. Parlee, M. B., 1973. "The premenstrual syndrome." *Psychol. Bull.* 80, 454–65.

96. Persky, H., 1974. "Reproductive hormones, moods and the menstrual cycle." Pp. 455–66 in Friedman, R. C. (ed.), *Sex Differences in Behavior*. New York: Wiley.

97. Phoenix, C. H., 1974. "Prenatal testosterone in the nonhuman primate and its consequences for behav-

ior." Pp. 19–32 in Friedman, R. C. (ed.), *Sex Differences in Behavior*. New York: Wiley.

98. Phoenix, C. H., R. W. Goy, and J. A. Resko, 1968. "Psychosexual differentiation as a function of androgenic stimulation." Pp. 33–49 in Diamond, M. (ed.), *Perspectives in Reproduction and Sexual Behavior*. Bloomington: Indiana University Press.

99. Potts, D. M., 1970. "Which is the weaker sex?" *J. Biosoc. Sci., Suppl.* 2, 147–57.

100. Ramey, E. R., 1973. "Sex hormones and executive ability." *Ann. N.Y. Acad. Sci.* 208, 237–54.

101. Reba, R. C., D. B. Cheek, and F. C. Leitnaker, 1968. "Body potassium and lean body mass." Pp. 165–81 in Cheek, D. B. (ed.), *Human Growth*. Philadelphia: Lea and Febiger.

102. Reinberg, A., and M. H. Smolensky, 1974. "Circatrigintan secondary rhythms related to hormonal changes in the menstrual cycle." Pp. 241–58 in Ferin, M., F. Halberg, R. M. Richart, and R. L. Vande Wiele (eds.), *Biorhythms and Human Reproduction*. New York: Wiley.

103. Richter, C. P., 1968. "Periodic phenomena in man and animals: their relation to neuroendocrine mechanisms (a monthly or near monthly cycle)." Pp. 284–309 in Michael, R. P. (ed.), *Endocrinology and Human Behaviour*. London: Oxford University Press.

104. Rosenblatt, J. S., 1965. "Effects of experience on sexual behavior in male cats." Pp. 416–39 in Beach, F. A. (ed.), (Conference on) *Sex and Behavior*. New York: Wiley.

105. Rosenblum. L. A., 1974. In discussion of section on "Effect of Hormones on the Development of Behavior." P. 79 in Friedman, R. C. (ed.), *Sex Differences in Behavior*. New York: Wiley.

106. Rossi, A. S., 1973. "Maternalism, sexuality, and the new feminism." Pp. 145–73 in Zubin, J., and J. Money (eds.), *Contemporary Sexual Behavior: Critical Issues in the 1970s*. Baltimore: The Johns Hopkins University Press.

107. Roth, M., and J. R. B. Ball, 1964. "Psychiatric aspects of intersexuality." Pp. 395–443 in Armstrong, C. N., and A. J. Marshall (eds.), *Intersexuality in Vertebrates Including Man*. New York: Academic Press.

108. Russell, G. F. M., 1972. "Premenstrual tension and 'psychogenic' amenorrhea: psycho-physical interactions." *J. Psychosom. Res.* 16, 279–87.

109. Sackett, G. P., 1974. "Sex differences in rhesus monkeys following varied rearing experiences." Pp. 99–122 in Friedman, R. C. (ed.), *Sex Differences in Behavior.* New York: Wiley.

110. Schmidt, G., and V. Sigusch, 1973. "Women's sexual arousal." Pp. 117–43 in Zubin, J., and J. Money (eds.), *Contemporary Sexual Behavior: Critical Issues in the 1970s.* Baltimore: The Johns Hopkins University Press.

111. Sears, R. R., 1965. "Development of gender role." Pp. 133–63 in Beach, F. A. (ed.), (Conference on) *Sex and Behavior.* New York: Wiley.

112. Shader, R. I., A. DiMascio, and J. Harmatz, 1968. "Characterological anxiety levels and premenstrual libido changes." *Psychosomatics* 9, 197–98.

113. Smolensky, M. H., A. Reinberg, R. E. Lee, and J. P. McGovern, 1974. "Secondary rhythms related to hormonal changes in the menstrual cycle: special reference to allergology." Pp. 287–306 in Ferin, M., F. Halberg, R. M. Richart, and R. L. Vande Wiele (eds.), *Biorhythms and Human Reproduction.* New York: Wiley.

114. Sommer, B., 1973. "The effect of menstruation on cognitive and perceptual-motor behavior: a review." *Psychosom. Med.* 135, 515–34.

115. Southam, A. L., and F. P. Gonzaga, 1965. "Systemic changes during the menstrual cycle." *Amer. J. Obstet. Gynecol.* 91, 142–65.

116. Staples, R., 1973. "Male-female sexual variations: functions of biology or culture." *J. Sex. Res.* 9, 11–20.

117. Stein, Z., and M. Susser, 1967. "Social factors in the development of sphincter control." *Dev. Med. Child Neurol.* 9, 692–706.

118. Stoller, R. J., 1968. *Sex and Gender.* New York: Science House.

119. Stoller, R. J., 1973. "Psychoanalysis and physical intervention in the brain: the mind-body problem again." Pp. 339–50 in Zubin, J., and J. Money (eds.), *Contemporary Sexual Behavior: Critical Issues in the*

1970s. Baltimore: The Johns Hopkins University Press.

120. Swyer, G. I. M., 1968. "Clinical effects of agents affecting fertility." Pp. 161–72 in Michael, R. P. (ed.), *Endocrinology and Human Behaviour*. New York: Oxford University Press.

121. Theilgaard, A., 1972. "Cognitive style and gender role in persons with sex chromosome aberrations." *Dan. Med. Bull.* 19, 276–82.

122. Vessey, M. P., 1972. "Gender differences in the epidemiology of non-neurological disease." Pp. 203–13 in Ounsted, C., and D. C. Taylor (eds.), *Gender Differences: Their Ontogeny and Significance*. Baltimore: Williams and Wilkins.

123. Washburn, S. L., and D. A. Hamburg, 1968. "Aggressive behavior in Old World monkeys and apes." Pp. 458–78 in Jay, P. C. (ed.), *Primates: Studies in Adaptation and Variability*. New York: Holt, Rinehart & Winston.

124. Whalen, R. E., 1974. "Sexual differentiation: models, methods and mechanisms." Pp. 467–81 in Friedman, R. C. (ed.), *Sex Differences in Behavior*. New York: Wiley.

125. Yalom, I. D., R. Green, and N. Fisk, 1973. "Prenatal exposure to female hormones: effect on psychosexual development in boys." *Arch. Gen. Psychiat.* 28, 554–61.

126. Young, W. C., 1961. "The hormones and mating behavior." Pp. 1173–1239 in Young, W. C. (ed.), *Sex and Internal Secretions*. Baltimore: Williams and Wilkins.

127. Zarrow, M. X., V. H. Denenberg, and B. D. Sachs, 1972. "Hormones and maternal behavior in mammals." Pp. 105–34 in Levine, S. (ed.), *Hormones and Behavior*. New York: Academic Press.

IV. AN ANTHROPOLOGICAL PERSPECTIVE ON SEX ROLES AND SUBSISTENCE

JUDITH K. BROWN

Introduction

It has been the mission of anthropology to enlarge the definition of "human nature" to include practices, beliefs, and values which are customary in societies other than our own. This widened perspective vastly complicates the question whether the "natural" roles of men and women are based on biological differences, on cultural elaborations of these differences, or on culturally determined learning. Cultural anthropologists have largely concentrated on identifying the latter two influences on sex role behavior.

This focus is exemplified in Margaret Mead's classic *Sex and Temperament in Three Primitive Societies* (16). Her field work among three New Guinea tribes, living within a radius of 100 miles, demonstrated that the sex roles which appear "natural" in our own society do not pertain universally. Both sexes may display behavior which in our society would be appropriate to only one sex, or the role of the sexes may appear reversed. Clearly these data call for a cultural rather than a biological explanation.

Further support for this position derives from the anthropological literature, which describes a wide range of customs related to sex roles. Many of these practices may at first appear inexplicable. Thus, for example, O'Brien (22) has assembled data from a variety of African societies in which marriage between women is practiced. She suggests that where this institution exists, it is not motivated by homosexuality. Rather, a "female husband" may be acting as a surrogate for an absent or deceased male kinsman. Alternatively, a "female husband" may improve her own status by being the sociological father of the children of her wife or wives.

The *couvade*, a custom which is widespread among the tribes of South America, has long puzzled anthropologists. In societies which practice the *couvade*, the husband seems to imitate or to partake in the birth process. Or the father's involvement in the birth of his child may take the form of observing prescribed magico-religious practices. Munroe, Munroe, and Whiting (18) have recently suggested that the *couvade* is the result of an underlying cross-sex identity.

In our own society, high political offices are rarely held by women, and such positions are considered inappropriate for the mothers of infants or very young children. Yet Hoffer (12) reports that among the Mende and Sherbro tribes of Sierra Leone, not only was there a tradition of women rulers, but their political position was enhanced by motherhood.

A final example suggests that in one North American Indian tribe, a well-defined and narrowly prescribed female role could be circumvented, provided a woman had the requisite qualifications and personality traits. Lewis (15) reports that among the North Piegan, women were expected to be submissive and retiring. However, a few older, wealthy women attained the quality of "manly-heartedness." Such women were not masculine. Rather, they were favorite wives, actively sexual and bold in their behavior. These women were also economic assets to their husbands. Regarded with some ambivalence, manly-hearted women enjoyed the prerogatives of an institutionalized alternative to the traditional female role prescribed by their society.

These illustrations suggest that there is marked variation in the cultural interpretation of sex roles. Some customs, such as the "female husband" and the *couvade* are without institutionalized analogues in our own society. Mead's data from New Guinea and Hoffer's data from West Africa suggest that our own interpretation of sex roles may be contradicted by the customary behavior in other societies. And the data on the manly-hearted woman suggest that contradictions in the interpretation of sex roles may exist side by side within the same society. Such examples could be multiplied. They serve to illustrate the fascinating complexity of the cultural or learned aspects of sex role behavior.

But anthropology is not a butterfly collection of the exotic. It seeks to discover regularities in human behavior which apply to all of mankind, and further, to discover the laws which govern these regularities. Thus it is a universal rule that the roles assigned to men and women differ. Yet in anthropology there is an exception to every rule, and so there are exceptions to this one. For example, in societies which practice male initiation rites, the dichotomy is not male/female. Instead one category includes all initiated men, and the other includes women, children, and uninitiated males. This dichotomy applies particularly to the practice of sacred rituals, which must be kept secret from the second category of persons. Another exception found in some societies is a dichotomy in which one category includes all women with child care responsibilities and the other category includes all men and those women not occupied with child care. This dichotomy applies to activities connected with the food quest (27). Thus even the definition of male and female, a major criterion for categorizing people in all societies, receives cultural elaborations which apply to certain aspects of life. A simple biological definition is not applied universally.

Within anthropology, there has been a tremendously increased interest in the study of sex roles in recent years. Since it is not possible to review this considerable literature fully, the present paper will concern itself with only one of its aspects: research concerned with the roles of the sexes in subsistence activities. (For an older but more inclusive review, the reader is referred to D'Andrade [8].)

Sex Roles in Subsistence

Subsistence activity in tribal and peasant societies includes one or more of the following: gathering wild vegetable foods, hunting small game, hunting large game, gathering marine foods, coastal fishing, deep-sea fishing, hunting of sea mammals, care of small domestic animals, herding large domestic animals, trading, and a variety of forms of cultivation.

Every society practices a division of labor by sex which pertains to subsistence activities. The assignment of tasks varies from society to society, yet as Murdock and Murdock and Provost (19, 20) have shown, this assignment is far from random. A society may depend upon its men to perform any of the subsistence activities enumerated above, and men typically make the predominant contribution to subsistence. However, there are numerous societies in which women make a predominant contribution. When this is the case, the society depends almost entirely upon gathering or hoe cultivation. The subsistence activities of men range more broadly than those of women. Yet societies like the Nsaw of Africa (13) depend almost entirely upon the subsistence activities of women. Women may also make a lesser contribution or no contribution, as among the Rājpūts of India (17).

The division of labor by sex as it pertains to subsistence activities has been explained by a variety of hypotheses. The first involves an explanation based upon the physical differences between the sexes. Some authors have suggested that the superior strength of men qualifies them for more strenuous work and for activities which take the participant farther from home, like hunting and deep-sea fishing. Because women are weaker and occupied with child care, they do the less strenuous, nondangerous work near home, such as tending the garden and caring for small domestic animals.

A second group of authors has suggested that the division of labor is best explained by psychological differences between the sexes. Domineering men compel women to perform the dull, laborious tasks, while they reserve the excitement of the hunt for themselves. Alternatively, women are considered better able to perform monotonous, repetitive tasks, while men are believed to excel at work that requires sudden bursts of energy.

Both the physiological and the psychological explanations are unacceptable as they stand, for they fail to account for contradictory evidence. A few examples must suffice: some Siberian Chukchee women have participated in the herding of reindeer. The trading activities of some West African women require travel of hundreds of miles. And in industrialized societies, many men are occupied with dull, repetitive work. The division of labor by sex does not seem to be based upon immutable sex-linked characteristics.

A somewhat fanciful explanation of the division of labor by sex was offered by Durkheim (9). He speculated that among "primitive" peoples, men and women were alike in physical strength and intelligence. The sexes were economically independent and their family ties were therefore "ephemeral." As civilization advanced, women became weaker and their brains became smaller. They depended more and more upon men, and thus the family became a more stable institution. In short, as women declined, civilization flourished.

Durkheim's idea that the economic relationship of the sexes is a major basis of the nuclear family has been more recently elaborated by Lévi-Strauss (14). He argued that the division of labor by sex should be viewed as a series of culturally imposed prohibitions, which assign tasks to one sex only, interdicting them to the opposite sex. Thus the sexes are made to depend on each other and marriage is strengthened by economic necessity. The rules which are the division of labor by sex make marriage necessary, just as incest rules make it necessary to enlarge the kinship unit by marriage outside the immediate family. Since the division of labor in many societies assigns complementary tasks to the sexes, there is some support for Lévi-Strauss's view. Furthermore, recent evidence shows that the interdependence of the sexes is maintained even in those few societies in which the division of labor is markedly uneven (6). However, the tasks assigned to men and women do not vary randomly, as Lévi-Strauss's view would suggest. The hypothesis fails to explain why only a limited number of subsistence activities are performed by women, whereas the work of men takes a variety of forms.

Yet another point of view concerning the division of labor by sex is presented by Brown (5). Noting that the division of labor by sex is universal but that the subsistence contribution by women is highly variable, she suggests that this variability derives from the dual role which women perform. In all societies, women have the major role in the care of children. Thus to maximize the subsistence role of women, their child-caring activities must be reduced, or alternatively, subsistence tasks must be compatible with simultaneous child care.

The first of these alternatives is familiar to us. In industrial or industrializing societies, the employment of women is made possible through schools and child care centers, which free women from child care responsibilities. In industrialized societies, debate concerning the employment of women tends to focus on the quality and availability of such substitute care. In tribal societies, the custom of having a child nurse or the institutionalized co-operation of female kin may free women for productive activities.

Yet in many tribal societies, women make a substantial contribution to subsistence without depending upon substitute care for their children. This is made possible because child care and subsistence activities are sufficiently compatible to be carried out simultaneously. This is the case when the work is such that it can be interrupted and easily resumed, does not require rapt concentration, is not dangerous, and can be carried out near home. Obviously subsistence activities such as hunting, deep-sea fishing, and the herding of large animals are not compatible with simultaneous child watching; gathering and hoe cultivation are.

Hence this hypothesis suggests an explanation for the fact that women contribute varying amounts to the subsistence activities of different societies, and for the fact that women's subsistence activities are restricted to a narrow range. Unlike other views which explain the division of labor on the bases of sex-linked physiology and/or psychology, this hypothesis can accommodate exceptions. Although no entire society depends upon women hunters and herders, individual women sometimes perform these activities if they are not caring for children. Thus among the Chukchee, the women who helped in the strenuous summer herding were women without children. And West African women traders who travel great distances are typically older women with grown children. Further indirect support for this position comes from a study of the practices related to infant care in a large number of societies (1). The findings suggest that fathers participate less in infant care in those societies in which male subsistence activities are incompatible with child care, such as herding and hunting of large animals.

The attempt to explain the varying subsistence contribution of women is complemented by a study by Ember and Ember (10) which attempts to explain the varying subsistence contribution of men. This they attribute to warfare, which is everywhere a predominantly male activity. They write: "In short, our hypothesis is that men will do more than women in subsistence unless warfare prevents them from doing so (10:579)." According to the authors, evidence gathered from many societies all over the world suggests that typically men make a dominant contribution to subsistence. They ascribe this to the fact that women have child care and household responsibilities, which prevent them from being full-time providers. It is only when warfare interferes with the subsistence work of men, and such warfare is frequent, that women will make a dominant contribution.

A recent paper by Sanday (25) seeks to synthesize the ideas of Brown, Ember and Ember, and Boserup (2). On the basis of quantified data, collected on a large sample of societies from all over the world, Sanday states:

> Where defense or related activities draw on a large proportion of male energy, the likelihood of females entering the subsistence sphere in some capacity increases. This likelihood can also increase independently when the conditions of the natural environment favor the successful utilization of female energy (25:1683).

The latter conditions pertain when shifting cultivation
or horticulture (as opposed to other forms of cultivation) are practiced and in tropical and subtropical settings, particularly in Sub-Sahara Africa and the Pacific
islands. Sanday suggests that historical factors may account for the similarity in the division of labor among
cultures found in the same major regions of the world.
But she notes that shifting cultivation is particularly
compatible with child care responsibilities, and that
shifting cultivation performed by women is appropriate
for certain environments and population densities.

The relationship between environment and the division of labor has also been explored by Hiatt for
hunter-gatherer societies. Here the relative contribution
by women to subsistence depends upon latitude. Hiatt
writes:

> The male contribution to the subsistence base in
> hunting societies is always substantial, ranging from
> a little less than half in the tropics to nearly 100 per
> cent in the arctic; the female contribution ranges
> from a negligible amount in the arctic regions to a
> substantial amount, but nowhere near 100 per cent,
> in the tropics (11:7).

It is the availability of gatherable foods which determines the contribution of women. The important contribution by men to hunter-gatherer subsistence is inter-
preted as a constant. Even in those societies in which
women make the greater contribution quantitatively,
the hunted meat contributed by the men is highly val-
ued and the importance of hunting is culturally stressed.

Thus hypotheses regarding the division of labor by
sex have varied greatly. Some anthropologists have
tended to emphasize the purely cultural determinants:
the subsistence base, the prevalence of warfare, and the
compatibility of subsistence activities with child care.
Some anthropologists have attempted to explain these

cultural arrangements on the basis of environmental variables. The introduction of quantified data based on the analysis of societies from all over the world has lent greater credibility to some of the proposed hypotheses. Explanations of the division of labor by sex on the bases of sex-linked physiological and psychological factors have recently become less acceptable to most anthropologists, and have been relegated by many to the realm of speculation.

The division of labor by sex has important implications for other aspects of culture: customs related to diet; social organization, particularly as it applies to work groups; and aspects of social and economic change. Below we will briefly consider recent work which relates the subsistence role of women to their position in society and to aspects of child rearing.

Implications for Child Rearing

Both Nerlove (21) and Brown (7) have suggested that just as the subsistence role of women must accommodate to the demands of child care, so child rearing must accommodate to the economic role of women. Nerlove's paper deals with infant care, while that of Brown deals with the rearing of children.

Nerlove's study was based upon extensive cross-cultural data. She found that when mothers make a major contribution to subsistence, supplementary foods are introduced into the diets of infants before they are one month old. Societies in which women do not participate as fully in subsistence are characterized by the later introduction of supplementary foods into infant diets. Nerlove suggests that the former infant feeding practices may result in poorer infant health and higher infant mortality.

Substantial female contribution to subsistence also appears to affect the nature of child-rearing practices applied to older children. A number of previous studies suggest that the mother must be able to depend on her children even when they are not closely supervised by her. Hence she will stress obedience, for the busy mother will not have time to be permissive and indulgent. She expects help from her children, and their work must be carried out responsibly, since the welfare of the household is at stake (7).

The initiation of adolescent girls is a dramatic socializing technique, which is typically practiced by societies in which women make a dominant contribution to subsistence (3). These initiation ceremonies are often complex and serve a variety of purposes. They may include tests of competence and periods of instruction. Although girls often have already mastered the skills they will need as providers, initiation rites are believed to instill the proper attitudes toward work.

Not only does the subsistence role of women influence the techniques of child rearing, but the training which girls receive prepares them for their future work. On the basis of data collected in seven societies, Whiting and Edwards (26) have recently suggested that girls are interrupted more than boys and further that the tasks assigned to girls must be performed near the home, unlike those assigned to boys. As noted above, two characteristics of the work of women are that tasks are interruptible and performed near home. Whiting and Edwards emphasize that task assignment and interaction with different categories of people (e.g., infants, and adults as opposed to peers) probably account for sex differences in child behavior. They write:

All of the behaviors that are characteristic of males and females seem remarkably malleable under the impact of socialization pressures, which seem to be

remarkably consistent from one society to another
. . . (26:171).

The Position of Women in Society

Numerous authors have suggested that the role of
women in production is related to their status in society.
Although this is an inviting hypothesis, it presents
difficulties in defining female "status," "power," or "position" in society. Only a few of the relevant studies will
be cited below.

Traditional Iroquois society is regarded by anthropologists as one in which women had an unusually high
position. Iroquois women could not serve in the highest
political offices of the tribe, but they did have considerable influence in the selection of those men who did.
Women were able to hold religious offices, and they had
authority within the household. Although Iroquois
women played a major role in the subsistence activities
of the tribe, Brown (4) has suggested that it was not
simply their contribution to the production of food
which accounted for their position. Rather it was the
control which Iroquois women retained of the entire
economic organization of the society.

In a paper which reinterprets Engels in the light of
ethnographic and historical data, Sacks (24) has
devised a complex scheme for analyzing the position of
women in four African tribes. Engels had suggested that
the position of women declined with the development
of private property and the separation of the family and
the community as economic units. Sacks argues that
"Women are social adults where they work collectively
as part of a productive group larger than or separate
from their domestic establishment" (24:218–219). Only
as social adults, recognized as such beyond the house-

hold, can women achieve equality. Sacks suggests that it is not simply the subsistence role of women which determines their position. It is determined by the organization of productive activities and the economy itself. Using a totally different theoretical framework and a world-wide sample of societies, Oliver (23) similarly suggests that female organization interacts with productivity to determine the power of women.

Using a small sample of societies, representing each of the major culture areas of the world, Sanday (25) found that the subsistence role of women was necessary but not sufficient to explain their status. The status of women was scaled on the following dimensions:

    I. Female control over produce
    II. External or internal demand or value placed on female produce
    III. Female participation in at least some political activities
    IV. Female solidarity groups devoted to female political or economic interests (25:1694)

Each of these studies suggests that there is no simple relationship between the subsistence role of women and their position in society. The organization of the economy and the presence of female groups beyond the domestic unit must be considered in determining the status of women. Finally, there is no consensus on the definition of feminine status.

Summary and Conclusion

We have examined one aspect of sex role research in anthropology: the division of labor by sex as it pertains to subsistence activities. Because this division of labor is found universally, and because the assignment of work by sex does not appear to be random, it is tempting to explain the phenomena on the bases of sex-linked physiology and/or psychology. Recent explanations have not taken this approach, however. Cultural factors have been suggested, and these in turn have been traced to environmental conditions. One might almost say that sex role research in the area of subsistence activities has moved into an era of environmental determinism. This trend applies to other areas of anthropological research as well.

The implications of the role of women in subsistence have also been examined briefly in terms of its impact on the socialization of children and on the status of women. Various hypotheses have been offered in this area of inquiry, and it is now evident that no simple interpretation can be adequate. The debate has been fruitful over the past few years, and we can expect new understanding to develop as research continues.

References

1. Barry, Herbert III, and Leonora M. Paxson, 1971. "Infancy and Early Childhood: Cross-Cultural Codes 2." *Ethnology* 10, 466–508.

2. Boserup, Ester, 1970. *Woman's Role in Economic Development*. London: George Allen and Unwin.

3. Brown, Judith K., 1963. "A Cross-Cultural Study of Female Initiation Rites." *American Anthropologist* 65, 837–53.

4. ———, 1970. "Economic Organization and the Position of Women among the Iroquois." *Ethnohistory* 17, 151–67.

5. ———, 1970. "A Note on the Division of Labor by Sex." *American Anthropologist* 72, 1073–78.

6. ———, 1973. "Leisure, Busywork and Housekeeping: A Note on the Unequal Division of Labor by Sex." *Anthropos* 68, 881–88.

7. ———, 1973. "The Subsistence Activities of Women and the Socialization of Children." *Ethos* 1, 413–23.

8. D'Andrade, Roy G., 1966. "Sex Differences and Cultural Institutions." Pp. 174–204 in Maccoby, Eleanor E. (ed.), *The Development of Sex Differences,* Stanford, California: Stanford University Press.

9. Durkheim, Émile, 1893. *De la Division du Travail Social.* (Reference here is to the 1933 edition: The Division of Labor in Society. George Simpson, trans. Glencoe: The Free Press.)

10. Ember, Melvin, and Carol R. Ember, 1971. "The Conditions Favoring Matrilocal versus Patrilocal Residence." *American Anthropologist* 73, 571–94.

11. Hiatt, Betty, 1970. "Woman the Gatherer." Pp. 2–8 in Gale, Fay (ed.), "Woman's Role in Aboriginal Society." *Australian Aboriginal Studies* No. 36. Social Anthropology Series No. 6. Canberra: Australian Institute of Aboriginal Studies.

12. Hoffer, Carol P., 1972. "Mende and Sherbro Women in High Office." *Canadian Journal of African Studies* 4 (2), 151–64.

13. Kaberry, Phyllis, 1952. "Women of the Grass Fields: A Study of the Economic Position of Women in Bamenda, British Cameroons." *Colonial Research Publication* 14. London: Her Majesty's Stationery Office.

14. Lévi-Strauss, Claude, 1956. "The Family." Pp. 261–85 in Shapiro, Harry L. (ed.), *Man, Culture and Society.* New York: Oxford University Press.

15. Lewis, Oscar, 1941. "Manly-Hearted Women among the North Piegan." *American Anthropologist* 43 (2), 173–87.

16. Mead, Margaret, 1935. *Sex and Temperament in Three Primitive Societies.* New York: Morrow.

17. Minturn, Leigh, and John T. Hitchcock, 1963. "The Rājpūts of Khalapur, India." Pp. 201–361 in Whiting, Beatrice B. (ed.), *Six Cultures: Studies of Child Rearing.* New York: Wiley.

18. Munroe, Robert L., Ruth H. Munroe, and John W. M. Whiting, 1973. "The Couvade: A Psychological Analysis." *Ethos* 1 (1), 30–74.

19. Murdock, George Peter, 1937. "Comparative Data on the Division of Labor by Sex." *Social Forces* 15, 551–53.

20. Murdock, George Peter, and Caterina Provost, 1973.

"Factors in the Division of Labor by Sex: A Cross-Cultural Analysis." *Ethnology* 12, 203–25.

21. Nerlove, Sara B., 1974. "Women's Workload and Infant Feeding Practices: A Relationship with Demographic Implications." *Ethnology* 13, 207–14.

22. O'Brien, Denise, 1972. Female Husbands in African Societies. Paper presented at the Meetings of the American Anthropological Association. Toronto.

23. Oliver, Pamela Elaine, 1972. "Women and Men in Social Exchange: A Cross-Cultural Study." Unpublished Masters' Thesis. University of North Carolina, Chapel Hill.

24. Sacks, Karen, 1974. "Engels Revisited: Women, the Organization of Production, and Private Property." Pp. 207–22 in Rosaldo, Michelle, and Louis Lamphere, (eds.), *Woman, Culture and Society*. Stanford, California: Stanford University Press.

25. Sanday, Peggy R., 1973. "Toward a Theory of the Status of Women." *American Anthropologist* 75, 1682–1700.

26. Whiting, Beatrice, and Carolyn Pope Edwards, 1973. "A Cross-Cultural Analysis of Sex Differences in the Behavior of Children Aged Three through Eleven." *The Journal of Social Psychology* 91, 171–88.

27. Williams, Sharlotte Neely, 1973. "The Argument Against the Physiological Determination of Female Roles: A Reply to Pierre L. van den Berghe's Rejoinder to Williams' Extension of Brown's Article." *American Anthropologist* 75, 1725–28.

V. SOCIAL INFLUENCES
ON SEX DIFFERENCES IN BEHAVIOR

VIVIEN STEWART

Introduction

"Women are what we have required them to be" wrote
John Stuart Mill in 1869 (55). A century later there is
still widespread agreement as to what the society expects women (and men) "to be" (13, 14); yet the contemporary feminist movement has made us so aware of
the malleability of what were once considered "eternal
verities" that the impact of social forces on sex
differences in behavior hardly seems to require docu-
mentation. However, while the broad directions of sex-
role socialization are familiar, the actual processes by
which babies born with male and female physical characteristics are transformed into "masculine" and "feminine" adults still contain many mysteries.

What effect does the mother have on the sex-role development of her child as compared with the father,
and what are the implications of this for the increasingly common phenomenon of the single-parent family?
What seems to be the relative influence of early as opposed to later experiences on the development of sex
differences in behavior, and what are the relative contributions of the family, school, media, and peers to this
process? Are girls under more pressure to conform to
appropriate sex-typed behavior than boys? Do social
class and race make a difference? And finally, is the
learner essentially a passive object shaped by these
larger forces, or does the learner in some way create the
very environment from which he/she learns? These are
some of the questions that need to be resolved. The re-

search literature on these subjects is vast, scattered, and reflects diverse theoretical approaches. It goes without saying that a chapter of this length cannot hope to rehearse all of the evidence for and against particular propositions. Rather it is an attempt to give a sense of our current knowledge about sex-role socialization processes and indicate where the puzzles still remain to be solved.

Sex Differences

In discussing the impact of social influences on sex differences, we are concerned with three broad sets of outcome variables, grouped together as ability, personality and interests. Under these category headings we would find the following:

Ability: General intelligence; verbal, numerical, spatial and analytical abilities; creativity; achievement.

Personality: Aggression, achievement motivation, emotional stability, passivity, dependence, activity level.

Interests: Interests, values, general orientation to life.

The last five years have witnessed an outpouring of studies attempting to pinpoint such differences. As with all large bodies of research the studies are of variable quality and there is more evidence on certain characteristics than others. There are also major gaps in the literature. Chapter IV points out the value of cross-cultural studies of sex differences, yet little attempt has been made to examine cultural differences within the United States in this respect. Sex differences in behavior in black families may vary greatly from those in white families, and class and income differences may also contribute significant variation which has not yet been systematically examined.

The studies that make up the existing literature vary widely in size and age of sample, methodology (e.g., self-report versus independent observation)* and magnitude of reported sex differences. For these reasons and because researchers approach the subject with different theoretical frameworks and with different operational definitions of concepts such as passivity, aggression, and the like, it is hard to regard many of the studies as strictly comparable with each other (39). Nevertheless certain sex differences have been consistently detected over the years and may therefore be thought reliably to exist, at least in those populations that have been studied. Of course this does not imply that they will continue to exist. *If* current concern about women's roles produces large-scale shifts in expectations and child-rearing behavior, then the nature of sex differences could be profoundly changed.†

Maccoby and Jacklin (51) have recently published an exhaustive review of more than two thousand studies of sex differences. They point out that many of the numerous sex differences reported in the literature are actually by-products of research on other subjects. They argue further that popular belief in sex differences has meant that any such findings of differences were likely to be reported in the literature whereas the absence of differences in any particular experiment was likely to go

---

* Since there is a high level of cultural agreement as to the appropriateness of certain kinds of behavior for each sex, independent observation is considered a more reliable methodology than self-reports, since these may reflect the prevailing cultural norms more than individual behavior. Nevertheless self-reports cannot be discounted, for if a woman believes, for example, that women are more fearful than men, then this is likely in itself to influence her behavior.

† This is an example of a problem common to much social research, namely that the phenomenon under study changes while it is being studied; sometimes the very act of studying it can cause the change.

unrecorded. Hence, basing their judgments on the more carefully designed research, Maccoby and Jacklin attempt to analyze which sex differences are myth, which real and which uncertain because inadequately tested.

Given the availability of their excellent study as well as earlier attempts to review the field, there seems no point (and indeed there would not be room) in a work of this kind in re-rehearsing the evidence for and against the existence of particular sex differences in the three categories listed above. Therefore we shall seek only to summarize briefly the general conclusions that can be drawn from the literature, and then to go on to devote most of this chapter to analyzing the complex social processes that appear to have a hand in the development of such differences.

Ability: There are no known differences between males and females in over-all intelligence. However, males have generally been found to excel in speed and co-ordination of gross bodily movements, mechanical comprehension, visual-spatial orientation, and quantitative reasoning. Females tend to excel in perceptual speed and accuracy, manual dexterity, memory, verbal fluency, and such mechanics of language as grammar and spelling. Only the difference in verbal ability is apparent in early childhood, since girls verbalize earlier than boys. Maccoby and Jacklin, disagreeing with previous writers, argue that the difference then disappears but reasserts itself at adolescence, with females consistently superior throughout high school on both "high-level" verbal tasks (analogies, comprehension of difficult material, creative writing) and "lower-level" measures (e.g., fluency and spelling). Some research reports sex differences in "mathematical" abilities, although the size of the sex difference varies from study to study. Such results are hard to interpret because mathematical problems often require several different skills including both visual-spatial and verbal. There seems no difference between the sexes in their early acquisition of quantitative skills but from adolescence on boys' "mathematical" skills increase faster than girls'. Maccoby and Jacklin note that the size of the variation in verbal and visual-spatial abilities in high school equals .25 and .40 of a standard deviation on average. However Messick (53) cautions that while all of these ability differences are statistically significant, it is difficult to establish which of them are of substantial magnitude primarily because the size of the observed differences may be more reflective of the measurement scale used and of differential experiences with test content than of any basic sex difference in underlying cognitive functioning.

Personality: The most commonly reported personality differences between the sexes are greater aggressiveness, activity level, achievement motivation and emotional stability in the male and a heightened social orientation in the female. Some general sex differences long thought to exist, such as passivity, dependency, conformity, fearfulness, and anxiety, have now been called into question either because direct observation does not confirm self-reports of differences in fear and anxiety (63) or because passivity, dependence and conformity have been shown to be a product of differential responses by the sexes to different situations (68).

In line with these findings, others have also suggested that female need-achievement has been underestimated, and that the use of different stimuli in the achievement motivation experiments would lead to an increase in girls' scores. Sex differences in activity level are found, but there is disagreement as to how early they can reliably be said to appear. Furthermore, since activity level is strongly affected by motivational state, it is hard to establish stable individual or group differences. Finally Maccoby and Jacklin have questioned whether girls are in fact more "social" than boys. While accepting that there may be sex differences in the kinds of social interaction engaged in, they point out that both sexes are equally interested in social stimuli and are equally adept at learning by imitating models (50).

In part such disputes reflect the greater problems of measurement in the personality domain (34). Definitional problems are also endemic. For example, Moyer (60) distinguishes eight different types of aggression, and his list does not exhaust the types of behavior discussed in the literature as "aggressive." All agree that boys exhibit more physical aggression and that this greater aggressiveness appears at an early age (about two years). Girls tend to engage in different types of aggression than boys, being more prone to use verbal rather than physical aggression. Even in this, however, Maccoby and Jacklin conclude that boys are more aggressive than girls.‡ Both sexes appear to become less aggressive with age although there are relatively few studies of aggression in adults.

As with measures of ability, personality variables also show wide variations within each sex and considerable overlap in the distribution of scores. However, there is some evidence to suggest that average sex differences

---

‡ These findings should not be taken to mean that girls cannot be highly aggressive. Since the distributions of characteristics between the sexes overlap, individual girls may be more aggressive than individual boys. In addition, Bandura has shown experimentally that groups of girls can be made to behave as aggressively as groups of boys. In a study of imitative aggression, he demonstrated that girls *learn* aggressive behavior to about the same degree as boys but that they are more inhibited about *performing* aggressive acts. However when persuaded that it was socially acceptable, girls exhibited the same amount of aggression as boys (3).

are somewhat greater for personality dimensions than for abilities and that they emerge rather earlier (53). Still, given the marked differences in the methods of measurement in the two domains, such generalizations should be viewed with extreme caution.

Interests and Values: The largest differences between the sexes are in their interest and values; in fact these differences are so great that they are used to construct scales and indices of masculinity and femininity for use in research and clinical practice (28).

In American society men tend to be more interested in scientific, mechanical, political, computational, and physically strenuous or adventuresome activities. Women tend to prefer literary, musical, artistic, social service, and sedentary activities. In studies of values, men score significantly higher on economic and political values and women on aesthetic, social and religious values. However, even on such measures of sex identification (masculinity/femininity scales), there is a fair amount of gender overlap. Bezdek and Strodtbeck (8), for example, reported that as many as 40 per cent of the persons in their samples displayed cross-sex preferences on particular sex-identification measures.

Learning of Behavior

The sex differences in ability, personality, and interests described heretofore represent a long tradition of biological and psychological research dating back to the turn of the century. Reflecting the influence of Freud, part of its purpose was the development of general masculinity and femininity scales aimed at understanding the emotional needs of both sexes and thus preventing neurosis (67). These scales are no longer accepted as valid, but the interest in defining and specifying the pre-

cise nature of sex differences remains. Biologists have
long sought explanations of such differences in the
different genetic and hormonal make-up of males and
females. Social scientists have also sought to account
for such differences, but with different conceptual
frameworks. Four major conceptual approaches can
be distinguished, one sociological and the other three
psychological. These perspectives are not mutually exclusive; many writers draw on all of them. However
they do point to different aspects of the socialization
process as crucial, so that it is useful to distinguish
among them.

To the sociologist a role is "the behavior expected of
an individual occupying a given social position" (32)
and the sex role one of the most significant to the individual psyche and to the society at large (59). Sex
differences in behavior are seen as being inculcated in
concert with the requirements of the role. This perspective holds that roles are continually reinforced throughout the life cycle by all the normal social processes of
approval, disapproval, reward, and punishment. On this
view, therefore, while the early years (including the
prenatal period) may possibly be critical for some
traits, it is difficult to estimate the impact of these early
influences since it is impossible to measure them in the
absence of later social controls which maintain the role
differences (30).

A modification of the roles perspective likens women
to a racial group in the sense that the role is
"ascribed"* and that the status of the role is low. (Both
males and females place lower value on the attributes of
the female than the male role [14].) On this view, pat-

---

* An ascribed role is one which its occupants acquire
automatically as a result of certain unchangeable characteristics such as sex or race. It is hence to be contrasted with
an "achieved" role.

terns of female behavior are seen as the product of social institutions dominated by males for whom "scientific" theories of biological determinism of behavior serve as ideological rationalizations for their superior status. Hence social processes are not neutral but reflect the distribution of power in the society; discrimination therefore becomes the central concept in the analysis of, for example, female lack of achievement (37).

A major problem for the roles perspective is that the connections between observed sex differences in behavior and adult sex roles are by no means always obvious. Spatial ability, for example, is a well-established sex difference, but spatial ability is not central to our concept of masculinity and femininity. Similarly sex differences in toy preferences can be found as early as age one, but at this age there does not seem to be a clear relationship between the toys that attract boys and girls and adult male and female activities. (Toy preferences that are clearly related to adult sex-typed activities do appear by preschool age, but the point remains that sex differences are found that cannot be explained simply by reference to anticipated adult roles.) As another example, the activities of preschool boys, which emphasize gross motor movements, clearly seem to foreshadow the later male interest in athletics; however the nature of the preschool motor activity of girls is not so clearly related to the future sex-typed activities of their school years (51).

The roles perspective links the existence of sex differences in behavior to the structures of the larger society, but does not examine in detail the processes by which sex differences in behavior come about. The psychological theories do attempt this. The first of these theories, that of selective reinforcement of behavior, is closely linked to the roles perspective. On this view, various socializing agents (parents, teachers, peers) reward sex-appropriate behavior (as defined by society's sex roles) and punish inappropriate behavior. However, while there are culturally approved differences in child-rearing practices, and while parents do punish some types of behavior that deviate from sex-role expectations (e.g., "sissy" behavior in boys), there are other areas of sex-differentiated behavior which parents do not seem to reward differentially by sex (e.g., aggression) (51).

The second and third of the psychological theories stress the importance of the child's imitation of adult models. Proponents of these theories point out that selective reinforcement alone could not account for the rate and breadth of sex-role stereotyping; some form of imitation must be involved. There is abundant evidence that children learn through observation; for example, they often tend to produce adults' inflections and mannerisms that have never been directly taught. Parents are usually considered the most likely models for imitation in the years before a child goes to school, since they are available, nurturant, and powerful vis à vis the child.

However, the undeniable existence of modeling behavior does not explain why children of different sexes learn different things, and here the two theories separate. One argues that children are exposed more frequently to models of the same sex; the other urges, by contrast, that children will imitate a same-sex model not because there is more frequent exposure to a same-sex model but because the child in some way perceives the same-sex model as similar to himself or herself. In other words, a child first develops a concept of what it is to be male or female and then tries to fit his own behavior to this concept.

In fact there seems to be little support for the notion

that boys develop male behavior because they are more frequently exposed to males while girls develop female behavior because of frequent exposure to females. In early childhood the mother is the most frequently available model for children of both sexes. (Hence the first of these two theories is compelled to argue that boys initially acquire feminine behavior and only later learn masculine behavior.) Then television makes available models of both sexes to both boys and girls. At a later age it is conceivable that fathers spend more of their free time with their sons, but there are few studies on this subject.

The second view, that children first develop a concept of their own gender identity and then begin to copy same-sex models, has been argued most strongly by Kohlberg (44). The development of a concept of gender is seen as a natural concomitant of the processes of cognitive development and maturation. Thus, Kohlberg argues that while children begin to label gender with partial accuracy at ages three to four, in keeping with the Piagetian timetable for the development of physical concepts their concept of gender identity does not become stable until age six. At that point the child forms an emotional attachment to the same-sex model and idealizes the characteristics of that model.

However, strong sex differences, such as sex-typed differences in toy preference, occur by ages three and four. Hence this perspective finds it difficult to account for those sex differences in behavior that appear before a child's gender concept has been formed. Further, if children do imitate their same-sex parent, then one might expect a daughter to resemble her mother in some respects and a son his father. This has not been found to be the case on non-sex-typed traits. Nor is there a significant correlation between a daughter's score on a femininity scale and her mother's (and similarly for males and masculinity scales). Unfortunately the evidence on this point is weak since it is difficult to say whether a measure of aggression in a five-year-old is measuring the same phenomenon as an aggression measure for an adult.

Psychoanalytic theory emphasizes the significance of cross-sex relationships between parents and children, and cross-sex modeling may be one of the complicating factors here. Clearly we need much more information in order to test these hypotheses as to the occurrence, range and timing of modeling behavior.

It is clear that the processes by which male and female babies become "boys" and "girls" are complex and that hypotheses about them currently outstrip the available empirical evidence. Further complications are added by the consideration that some traits may be more biologically influenced than others. Aggression might be one such trait, for example; if true, this might explain the somewhat puzzling finding of strong sex differences in aggressive behavior without clear and unequivocal evidence of selective reinforcement by parents. It is also now widely recognized that the acquisition and performance of behavior may be governed by different sets of factors. Finally, both sociology and psychology are moving away from the concept of an infant as a *tabula rasa,* the passive "recipient" of socializing influences, to a notion of adult-infant interaction as an essentially reciprocal process, in which the infant's characteristics may influence the behavior of its caretaker as well as vice versa.

The following sections discuss, in brief compass, our knowledge of the impact of various institutions, family, school, peers, and media on the development of sex differences in behavior. Given the limited space available in this chapter and the great significance placed upon academic achievement in modern industrial societies, the discussion will concentrate primarily on those skills and personality attributes considered significant for academic achievement.

The discussion will illustrate a major difference between human and nonhuman species, namely, the long length of the socialization period. Observations of sex differences have been made at many different points in the life cycle, but most empirical research has concentrated on early childhood and, because of the availability of subjects, on college students. Hence our discussions of other stages or aspects of socialization have of necessity to rely more on theoretical argument and inferences from other research than on studies directed specifically to this topic. In these cases the differing quality of the data is indicated and the conclusions are, in consequence, more tentative.

The Family

As with other aspects of research on sex differences, research on parenting behavior is not without its methodological flaws in the definition and measurement of phenomena, the tendency for working-class and other cultural groups to be excluded from samples, and so on (39). Moreover, following the previous discussion of the processes by which sex differences in behavior may be acquired, it is apparent that several different attributes of the parents may be relevant—their views on the gender-appropriateness of various behaviors, the extent to which their own behavior is sex-typed, and finally, how closely either of these is related to the way they treat their children. While studies use a variety of techniques to gather information and while some are based on parents' reports of their parenting behavior (a technique which is unreliable because it tends to reflect stereotypes rather than behavior), there does seem to be significant agreement among them that (1) there are substantial differences in the way parents treat children of different sexes, and that (2) different kinds of parental behavior are associated with high academic achievement for the two sexes.

Major differences in maternal behavior toward male and female infants appear within the first few weeks of a child's life. In the first six months boys are handled more frequently and more vigorously than females (in spite of the fact that female infants are sturdier) while mothers vocalize more to girls (39, 42, 47). The reasons for these marked differences are unknown, although the greater value placed on the male and the greater irritability of the male infant have both been invoked as explanations. It is probable that both the characteristics of male and female infants and the sex-role views of the mother are influential. Maternal behavior is not entirely a response to the infant, as has been demonstrated by several studies that have found a strong relationship between a mother's parenting behavior and her orientations prior to the child's birth. Nor is maternal behavior the sole determinant of the infant's behavior, as is indicated by the sex differences in tactile stimulation that have been found in infants less than four days old (39). An interaction hypothesis seems the most reasonable.

After six months of age there is an interesting shift in socialization, and girls receive more physical contact than boys (47). This "early weaning" of males has been held to contribute to their greater independence, a personality attribute considered vital for achievement.

Attempts to analyze the relationship between sex differences in infant socialization and later achievement orientation and behavior have hypothesized two important dimensions of parental behavior, warmth/hostility and permissiveness/restrictiveness (70). There are few

direct observational studies of parental warmth and
children's achievement, but data from a variety of
sources indicate an interesting sex difference. High *mental* nurturance and protection are related to high IQ for
boys only (4, 28). For girls achievement and academic
competence is related to lower maternal nurturance and
warmth (20, 21). There may be an optimal range of
parental warmth and protectiveness that is enough to
promote effective growth, but is not so smothering as to
inhibit some parent-child conflict which seems essential
for the development of independence. Within this optimal range the same parent behavior seems to have different effects on girls than boys.

We know that mothers in general report greater anxiety and protectiveness of their daughters than their
sons, an observation which, if true, might help to account for the lower academic achievement of females.
It does appear that those mothers who are perceived as
more rejecting have daughters who achieve more. Further, Baumrind (5, 6, 7) found that for girls, resistiveness to adults and peers was related to more achievement
orientation and purposive behavior, while for boys resistiveness was associated with less achievement behavior. However, while studies of early childhood have
found marked differences in maternal handling of boys
and girls, such as those described above, it is often difficult to translate these differences into a warmth/hostility dimension.

Perhaps the more crucial factors for children's
achievement are freedom from maternal restriction,
freedom to wander and explore, and encouragement of
independence. Permissiveness in a context of moderate
warmth is associated with independence in children,
while restrictiveness is associated with dependency and
passivity (70). The traditional view of this subject has
been that girls are subject to greater maternal restriction

and are hence more dependent and passive, qualities
unsuited to high academic achievement. However, recent data is conflicting as to whether girls are encouraged to be less exploratory and more dependent in
the first two years of life. Goldberg and Lewis (29)
found more proximity-seeking in girls at thirteen months
and more crying in a frustration situation, but Maccoby
and Jacklin (49) did not. Studies of activity level of infants are similarly inconclusive (58). In fact several
studies suggest that the activity level of infants is not a
stable characteristic and hence does not predict to later
individuals differences in behavior (50).

Studies of older children have sometimes suggested
that parents are in fact more restrictive with their sons
than their daughters. Parents do discipline their sons
more (6), but this is not necessarily the same as restrictiveness, and such punishment may constitute independ-
ence-training. The complexity of the issue is apparent.

Parents consistently report earlier granting of independence to and greater encouragement of achievement
in their sons, but there are a few direct observational
studies of this. We have noted that data on sex differences in dependency and exploratory behavior are
equivocal in the preschool years, but differences that do
not appear until later can have their roots in early experiences. Hence an important topic for further research is whether parents do indeed encourage independence and exploration less in girls.

Most of the studies of parent-child interaction in fact
deal with the behavior of the primary "caretaker," the
mother. However, recent observation studies provide
some evidence that fathers interact in a qualitatively
and quantitatively different manner than mothers (2),
although the patterns of, for example, vocalization toward infants are by no means simple and consistent.
There is indirect but suggestive evidence that fathers

may interact differentially with sons and daughters, being more apprehensive about their daughters' safety but more severe and concerned about achievement and competition with their sons. In general, research on father-child interaction is scanty, and only recently have we begun to accumulate data. Hence the consequences for sex-role socialization of what appears to be a current trend toward greater male participation in child rearing are currently unknown.

The likelihood that fathers treat children differently than do mothers raises questions as to the impact on sex-differentiated behavior of other aspects of modern family structure. The high rate of divorce, for example, has led to a large increase in the number of single-parent families. Currently about 30 per cent of the country's households are single-parent (26); 12 per cent of children (31.5 per cent of black children) under the age of eighteen are in single-parent families and many more have undoubtedly been through a period of single-parenting. Most single-parent families are headed by females, and the effects of father absence on children's perceptions of sex role and sex differences in behavior are summarized by Hetherington and Deur (36) as follows:

Father absence appears to be associated with a wide range of disruptions in social and cognitive development in children (1, 56), and the effects seem most severe if the father leaves home before the child is five. Not all studies of father absence have found effects on sex-typed aspects of personality or behavior, but those which have done so suggest that the effects may be different for boys than girls. Boys have been found to show feminized behavior during the preschool years, but these effects either disappear as they get older or else are transformed into "compensatory masculinity," an excessively assertive form of behavior (52). Girls, on the other hand, do not show any clear effects until adolescence, when they seem to have a variety of difficulties in responding appropriately in heterosexual situations (36). While such deviations from normal gender behavior do appear, there is considerable dispute as to their form, consistency, and cause. They seem to be modified to a significant extent by other factors such as an emotionally stable, loving mother who reinforces the child for appropriate sex-typed behavior; and there are strong reservations as to whether the effects can be attributed to father absence per se or whether they are really products of the stress likely to exist in "broken homes (64)."

Another striking feature of the modern family is the high rate of labor-force participation by married women. Approximately 40 per cent of women of working age are in the labor force today, including a third of all mothers with children under the age of six. There is a sizable body of research on working mothers, but it is hard to draw clear conclusions from it, since many studies do not control for social class, single-parent families, age at marriage, mother's employment history, parental attitudes toward work, etc. (71). A prevailing cultural bias against working mothers is also readily apparent (35).

The effects of working mothers on their children's sex-role stereotypes and sex-typed behavior are clearer for girls than for boys. Daughters of employed mothers perceive significantly smaller differences between men and women than do daughters of homemaker mothers. Daughters of working mothers have higher educational aspirations and are also more likely to pursue careers themselves (31). There are several ways in which maternal employment might affect children's stereotypes. Working may raise the self-concept of the mother, thus making her a more confident role model for her daughter. A working mother may not be at home for long enough periods to "overprotect" a daughter, thus encouraging higher achievement. Finally, maternal employment does lead to a different division of labor within the home and to more shared decision making, so that neither parent is modeling a highly stereotyped role (38).

School

Between the ages of five and six, the child enters school and another set of forces begins to operate. Until that point, the child's world has been defined largely by his family. The school is the child's first major experience with the society outside of the intimate environment of the home, and as such it is undoubtedly a powerful teacher of the norms governing secondary relationships. Within the home, the child's status is secure and relatively unchanging; the world outside is characterized by multiple forms of stratification, and status is allocated quite differently from that in the family. As modern society's major vehicle for selection into the adult occupational structure, it falls to the school to teach these processes.†

A precise estimate of the impact of school on the sex-role socialization of the child would require knowledge of how much of the appropriate behavior has been learned in the preschool years. As is the case with most aspects of child development, the relative significance of the early years as compared with later socialization is still a matter of dispute. We have seen that sex differences in many dimensions of behavior do manifest

---

† With the advent and spread of television, children have some opportunity to learn about the larger society before leaving the home; it is therefore possible that the school's role in teaching these processes has been somewhat reduced, or at least, modified.

themselves in infancy and the preschool years. Sex differences in aggression are apparent from about age two, and by ages five or six both sexes view the male role as more powerful. However, differences in visual-spatial ability are not found until the early school years, and the data on dependency and exploratory behavior are equivocal before age six.

While there have been no direct comparisons of the relative impact of home and school on the development of sex differences in behavior, in recent years studies of the relative contributions of school and family background to academic achievement have tempered some popular American myths as to the omniscience of education. Nevertheless such studies should not be construed (as they often have) to mean that schools "make no difference"‡ to children. Clearly they do, both through the formal curriculum and the social organization of the school, the "hidden" curriculum. The clear historical trend has been for the school to occupy more and more years of a student's life, taking over many socialization functions that formerly belonged to the family.

Studies of achievement indicate that the school's lessons are learned most effectively when they are in accord with the values of the family. Certainly in the learning of sex-role and sex-appropriate behavior, schools seem to convey the same standards as are held by most parents. By contrast with other countries where "character education" is an integral part of schools, American schools have tried (at least in their official pronouncements) to shy away from responsibility for teaching values. These are seen as the prerogative of the family and the church. Nevertheless, attitudes and values about sex roles are embedded in the curriculum,

---

‡ For a good summary of the debate, see Coleman (18).

whether crudely, as in the designation of some courses and extracurricular activities as being for males and others for females (65), or more subtly, in the assumptions underlying the design of vocational-interest tests (16), in the item content of achievement tests (73), in the number and nature of the stories about males and females contained in basic readers and other texts (15, 74), or in the lack of attention paid to women in history syllabi and notions about the appropriate role of women that permeate even seemingly technical subjects.

Some of these aspects of differential socialization in the schools are now breaking down under public pressure and, in some cases, court order. But others persist, and are perhaps harder to eradicate. As has been discussed in the previous section, it is now widely recognized that many complex behaviors are not directly taught but are learned through imitation or observation. Hence the social organization of schools (where 70 per cent of teachers are female, but 70 per cent of the elementary school principals, 97 per cent of the high school principals and 99 per cent of superintendents are male [62]) is likely to teach a powerful lesson about the authority structure of society in general and the relative roles of men and women in it.

Further, given the propensity for learning to take place through observation and imitation as much as through direct instruction, an important function of the school is the provision of a variety of adult role models. Of these probably the most significant is the classroom teacher. This is especially true in the elementary grades, where children spend most of the day with a single teacher. Virtually every person with whom an individual interacts for even a short period of time has the capacity to serve as a model for some aspect of behavior, although we know little about what variables help to determine which people become the objects of identification and modeling for whom. Teachers are presumed to be powerful models not simply because of the amount of teacher-pupil contact, but also because of their high status for the student derived in part from their ability to reward and punish different kinds of behavior.

It is consonant with this recognition of the teacher's importance that of all these aspects of sex-role socialization in school, only the role of the teacher has received sustained empirical attention. Still there is little systematic information on the sex-role stereotypes held by teachers. It is probably safe to assume, however, both from the widespread agreement on sex-role stereotypes and the rather conservative standards that govern the hiring of teachers, that they are similar to the population as a whole (46) in spite of the fact that many of them are working mothers whose place is clearly not "in the home."

In addition to any explicit instructions about sex roles teachers may impart as a reflection of their own value system, teachers also socialize boys and girls differently through generalized differences in interaction. A long tradition of research on teachers looked to their personal characteristics as predictors of their effectiveness, but such research told us little about classroom behavior or teaching effectiveness (57). Therefore more recent research turned to an analysis of actual classroom interaction. While teachers' interactions with students have not always been found to be related to the sex of the student (22), generally boys have been found to receive a higher level of negative feedback (54) or a higher level of both positive and negative feedback (12, 25, 69). In addition to "receiving" more teacher-initiated interaction, boys have been found to initiate more contacts with the teacher (19). Even when girls do volunteer, they are significantly less likely to be called upon (25). These findings are consonant with the results of several other studies which report that teachers tend to view girls in a more stereotyped way than boys. Teachers are able, for example, to give a more complex, differential and evaluative picture of the boys in their classroom than of the girls upon whom they tend to comment only in terms of friendly, agreeable behavior.

What has not been determined by this tradition of research is whether teachers' differential interactions with male and female students can be attributed more to the sex-role expectations held by the teachers and their consequent actions, or more to actual sex differences in behavior students bring to the classroom. Brophy and Good argue, for example, that the pace of activity in the classroom is such that the teacher's role is necessarily reactive rather than pro-active and that the higher level of teacher-boy interaction is therefore primarily a consequence of the more assertive behavior of boys in initiating interaction (12). However, more evidence will be necessary before this question can be settled.

Studies of teacher-pupil interaction do have significant technical deficiencies as a result of their lack of control for other key variables. Nevertheless, these observed differences in teacher-pupil interaction could be of considerable importance since the development of competence and achievement motivation is thought to depend on accurate and continuous feedback. Certainly girls in elementary school do show a tendency to underestimate their abilities and exhibit less persistence on a task and a greater tendency to avoid tasks than do boys (20, 21). In spite of these early suggestions of female underachievement, the marked sex differences in interaction discussed above have *not* been shown to be directly related to sex differences in achievement (12). One reason for this could be the short time-length of the studies. Another lies in other forces which affect the pattern of female achievement.

In elementary school, girls generally outperform boys in all subjects except mathematics. In fact the sex difference is so great that many educators have expressed concern about the "underachievement" of boys in elementary school. Throughout high school girls continue to earn better grades than boys in most subjects, but their performance on ability tests declines relative to that of boys, their confidence in their ability to do college work is less, and very few plan to major in science subjects (24). In addition, far fewer of them expect to be working in a professional occupation. Indeed of the brightest high school graduates who do not go to college, 75–90 per cent are women.

While a larger proportion of girls than boys graduate from high school, a smaller proportion of them go on to college. The switch in the relative performance of males and females is complete by the level of graduate school, as is illustrated by the fact that between 1960 and 1969 only 12 per cent of all doctoral degrees went to women. Since 1969 both the proportion of girls going on to college and the proportion of doctoral degrees awarded to women have risen, but the differences in male and female achievement patterns remain.

While the broad patterns of male and female performance are clear, the psychological mechanisms by which these changes come about are still uncertain. Boocock offers one explanation of these shifts in relative performance in terms of the relationship between personality and ability and, more specifically, in terms of an incongruence between the student role and the sex role for both boys and girls (9). For boys the atmosphere of the elementary school with its female teachers and its emphasis upon obedience and conformity instead of more active learning is feminine. Indeed reading is identified by children as a "feminine" subject (41). Boys do not catch up with girls in performance until the clear linkages of academic achievement with occupational and other kinds of adult success make the student role more clearly congruent with their male role. For girls such "feminine" traits as obedience and friendliness are apparently functional at the elementary level, but intellectual interests and potentialities are increasingly repressed as they come to represent "unfeminine" competitiveness and seem incompatible with their concern with interpersonal relationships.

A somewhat different explanation was suggested by the early studies of achievement motivation. The inability of the model used in these studies to account for variations in this attribute in females led some to conclude that women lacked achievement motivation, probably as a result of early childhood experiences. More recent work, however, has suggested that the female "need to achieve" has been considerably underestimated.

Horner (40) has postulated a "motive to avoid success" among bright women. This motive is seen as the internal psychological representation of the dominant societal stereotype which views intellectual achievement as inconsistent with femininity. However, other studies have failed to replicate her findings and have, in some cases, found the motive to avoid success as great among males as females. Hoffman (39) argues along somewhat different lines that female achievement efforts are instigated primarily by their needs for affiliation and desire for social approval, and that if achievement threatens affiliation, performance is likely to be sacrificed. However, Stein and Bailey (70), in their review of the literature, disagree with Hoffman's interpretation. Their view of the evidence suggests not that female achievement is instigated primarily by affiliation motives but that social skills are a central area of achievement concern for many females.

Thus the question remains open as whether there is a "flight from achievement" during adolescence or whether the goals of achievement-striving shift for many females. Whichever is the case, a powerful instrument in shaping and articulating these diverging paths of development in the high school and college years is the peer group.

Peer Groups

Bronfenbrenner, among others, has argued that the marked age segregation of American society, with sustained contact with the adult world limited to parents and teachers, makes peer groups and the media very significant socializing agents (11). While we know almost nothing about the effects of peer influence before puberty,* a large body of research over the last twenty years has documented the existence of a marked youth culture in adolescence (10, 23, 43).

A few writers have argued that the existence of such a subculture smacks of a self-fulfilling prophecy,† but most students of adolescence agree on its existence both in high school and college. What is not agreed upon is its strength and the extent to which it is separate from and in conflict with the school or the adult world.

Coleman's classic study of the American high school, *The Adolescent Society,* argued that the family's influence was declining relative to that of the peer group since the family had lost many of the economic

---

* The lack of research on this age group reflects the assumption that the family is the dominant socializing agency until adolescence.

† Musgrove, for example, writes: "Having invented the adolescent, society has been faced with two major problems: how and where to accommodate him in the social structure, and how to make his behavior accord with the specifications (61:33)."

and social functions it formerly possessed (17). Coleman's findings showed that academic performance was not an insignificant value in the peer culture, but it was not nearly as significant as athletic prowess for boys and popularity (especially with the opposite sex) for girls.

As has been clear throughout this chapter, one of the major problems of research on socialization is the difficulty of disentangling the effects of different socializing agents from one another. Coleman saw the peer group as emphasizing different, even conflicting, values from those of parents and the school. Such a conflict would yield distinct methodological advantages in that it would allow us to begin to make crude measurements of the relative strength of the two influences. However, no such conflict has yet been shown to exist in the learning of sex-appropriate behavior, and Coleman's findings have, in any case, been challenged and modified by later research. Brittain has argued that the values of the peer group are not as different from those of adults as Coleman had suggested (10), and that where cross-pressures do exist the relative salience of parents or peers depends upon the particular issue. Adolescents tend to turn to their parents for advice on problems of school work, educational plans for the future, and general moral decisions, but to their peers for help on interpersonal relations, popularity, and status with peers. Such arguments, while not directed specifically to the issue of sex roles, suggest that adolescents may learn different aspects of their gender roles from their peers than they do from their parents. It is also conceivable that the peer group may be more significant for boys than for girls. Maccoby and Jacklin suggest that boys are especially concerned with maintaining their status in their peer group and that they may therefore be more susceptible to pressure from the group (50). Then too, during childhood at least, girls tend to be more obedient to the commands of adults than boys. However, we do not know if this extends into adolescence, and for the present therefore the possibility of sex differences in the saliency of the peer group remains highly speculative.

Events may quickly render social science findings out of date, and the impact of the interest in women's roles may change the socializing "messages" of both parents and peers. Opinion polls now report significant generational differences in attitudes toward women's roles, with older women adhering to more traditional concepts of women's aspirations and behavior than younger women (33, 75). Opinion polls are but superficial evidence where deeply held values are concerned, but they do suggest that currently there may be some conflict between what parents teach and what peers teach about sex roles.

The relative effects of same-sex as opposed to different-sex peers are no better documented than is any other aspect of peer influence. We do know that high school males tend to hold lower aspirations for their female counterparts than do high school females, suggesting once again the critical role males may play in teaching expected female behavior. Evidence from some single-sex colleges also shows that higher proportions of female students go into "male" fields such as science where the peer group is all female rather than of mixed sex (72). Such findings are only suggestive at this point since this effect is not found consistently across all women's colleges, and even where it is found, it is difficult without further study to separate out the effects of self-selection from those of peer influence.

Media

By the age of four, most children will have spent between two and three thousand hours watching television
(according to a 1973 survey of the Nielsen company),
and children in general spend an average of twenty-
seven hours a week in front of the set. In terms of the
amount of time a child spends with it, the television
must rank as the family's closest rival and, given the
separation of home and work place in modern cities, it
is often the young child's major window onto the adult
world. It stands to reason that television must have a
major impact on children—at minimum through the
other activities it displaces. Yet apart from evaluations
of a few specifically educational programs (such as
"Sesame Street") and laboratory research on the effects
of television on violent behavior, there is little hard research evidence as to precisely what or how much children learn from television.

This is in large part a reflection of the acute
methodological difficulties of research in this area. The
fact that children select the programs they watch ren-
ders many comparisons invalid, while selective attention
to the program and selective identification with the
characters in it also makes measurement of its impact
difficult (48). Hence the evidence that does exist is
often complex and couched in terms not of how much
impact television has but rather of what effects it has on
what kinds of children under what circumstances. There
are currently no research answers to these questions
with regard to learning sex-appropriate behavior, but
one must assume that the smaller number of female
than male characters on children's television, the behavior they display, and the roles they play in cartoons,
films, and commercials do affect some children's devel-

oping view of the world and the sex roles within it. Beginning with Friedan, a number of authors have argued that the portrayal of women on television is highly stereotyped, that the roles shown for women do not reflect the variety of roles occupied by women in real life (27). This is consistent with evidence from other research which suggests that television does contribute to stereotyped thinking in children. Hence to the extent children acquire concepts of sex-appropriate behavior from television, it seems that they learn norms of behavior which are even more sharply sex-differentiated than those of society as a whole.

Conclusion

The thrust of this chapter has been to demonstrate the significance and complexity of social influences on the development of sex-typed behavior. We have also been concerned to show the limits and ambiguities of our present knowledge rather than provide simple answers to the tendentious questions frequently encountered on this subject.

Our account of the processes of sex-role socialization ends at early adulthood. Thus it reflects the assumption underlying most research on human development, namely that while the development of an idea of the self is never-ending, by the time of adulthood the concept is subject to less change. As a result of this assumption, there has been little systematic attention paid to the influences on adult development, and particularly female development, although there have been some studies of the careers of small groups of unusually successful women. Certainly the influences on sex differences in the behavior of adults warrant further attention.

It is only in the early childhood period that we have

detailed observational studies of sex differences in behavior, and paradoxically, it is here that the complex-
ities of the process become most apparent. Even for the
early childhood period some general notes of caution
need to be sounded about all of the studies. While some
were conducted in Europe, the vast majority of the
studies were undertaken on white, middle-class Americans in the 1950s and 1960s. Very few attempts have
been made to study the cultural variation that exists
even within the United States. Most of the studies were
conducted on relatively small samples, and definitional
problems abound. While there appears to be an
aggregate sex difference on many characteristics, the
actual distribution curves for males and females overlap
to a considerable extent.‡ Hence it is possible for individual women to be more "masculine" on some characteristics than some men. Thus whatever is true in
aggregate statistical terms, sex is an unreliable predictor
of behavior for *individual* men and women.

Discussions of the nature of sex differences tend to be
very time- and culture-bound (cf. Chapters IV and VI),
and even within the recent past there have been substantial changes in the role of women in the paid labor
force. Since this discussion is based on research done
over the last fifteen years, it may appropriately be asked
how relevant these findings are to the social influences
on children today. Under pressure from the new
feminists, various types of media are beginning to
change the ways in which they portray women, different
kinds of role models are more available to young girls,
and schools are slowly changing their curriculum re-

---

‡ If more studies were conducted on "working class"
populations, it is possible that larger sex differences would be
apparent, since there is some evidence that working-class
behavior is more sex-typed than that of the middle class
(45).

quirements. There is some evidence of a generational shift in sex-role stereotypes, and in addition, as we have suggested, actual behavior may not be as sex-typed as the stereotypes people subscribe to.

Yet several factors suggest that the forces indicated by our discussion will be relevant for some time to come. Not all sectors of the population voice a changed view of sex-role stereotypes. In addition, there is informal evidence that while there has been some shift in the language with which children talk about males and females, deeper probing shows that their conception of the adult role possibilities for males and females have not altered significantly. This is as might be expected, since conceptions of sex differences are deeply ingrained in the culture and such attitudes are hard to shift (66). Finally, current journalistic accounts suggest that in whatever shifts have taken place in attitudes toward sex roles, males have changed less than females. Since our account has suggested that males may play a crucial role in sex-role stereotyping, this also tends to support the view that the research of the last fifteen years is still relevant and that the processes dealt with in this chapter are very much in operation today.

References

1. Bacon, M. K., I. L. Child, and H. Barry, 1963. "A cross-cultural study of correlates of crime." *Journal of Abnormal Social Psychology.* 66, 291–300.
2. Ban, P., and M. Lewis, 1971. Mothers and fathers, girls and boys: attachment behavior in the one-year-old. Paper presented at the meeting of the Eastern Psychological Association, New York City.
3. Bandura, A., 1973. *Aggression: a social learning analysis.* Englewood Cliffs: Prentice-Hall.
4. Bardwick, J. M., 1971. *The psychology of women: a study of biosocial conflict.* New York: Harper & Row.

5. Baumrind, D., 1970. "Socialization and instrumental competence in young children." *Young Children.* December, 9–12.

6. ———, 1971. "Current patterns of parental authority." *Developmental Psychology Monograph.* 4. (1, Pt. 2)

7. ———, and A. E. Black, 1967. "Socialization practices associated with dimensions of competence in preschool boys and girls." *Child Development.* 38, 291–327.

8. Bezdek, W., and F. L. Strodtbeck, 1970. "Sex-role identity and pragmatic action." *American Sociological Review.* 35, 491–502.

9. Boocock, S. S., 1972. *An introduction to the sociology of learning.* New York: Houghton Mifflin.

10. Brittain, C. V., 1963. "Adolescent choices and parent-peer cross-pressures." *American Sociological Review.* 28, 385–90.

11. Bronfenbrenner, U. B., 1970. *Two worlds of childhood: USA USSR.* New York: Basic Books–Russell Sage Foundation.

12. Brophy, J. E., and T. L. Good, 1974. "Teacher-student relationships." *Causes and consequences.* New York: Holt, Rinehart & Winston.

13. Broverman, I. K., D. M. Broverman, and F. E. Clarkson, 1970. "Sex role stereotypes and clinical judgments of mental health." *Journal of Consulting and Clinical Psychology.* 34, 1, 1–7.

14. Broverman, I. K., S. R. Vogel, D. M. Broverman, F. G. Clarkson, P. S. Rosenkrantz, 1972. "Sex role stereotypes: a current appraisal." *Journal of Social Issues.* 28, 2, 60–78.

15. Chafetz, J. S., 1971. *Masculine-feminine or human? An overview of the sociology of sex roles.* Itasca, Illinois: F. E. Peacock.

16. Cole, N. S., 1973. "On measuring the vocational interests of women." *Journal of Counseling Psychology.* 20 (2), 105–12.

17. Coleman, J. S., 1961. *The adolescent society.* New York: Free Press.

18. ———, 1973. "Review symposium." *American Journal of Sociology.* 78 (6), 1523–44.

19. Cosper, W. B., 1970. "An analysis of sex differences in teacher-student interaction as manifest in verbal and nonverbal behavior cues." Unpublished Ed.D. disser-

tation. University of Tennessee. (Available from University Microfilms)

20. Crandall, V. J., 1964. "Achievement behavior in young children." *Young Children*. 20, 77–90.

21. ——, A. Preston, and A. Rabson, 1960. "Maternal reactions and the development of independence and achievement behavior in young children." *Child Development*. 31, 243–51.

22. Davis, O., and J. Slobodian, 1967. "Teacher behavior toward boys and girls during first grade reading instruction." *American Educational Research Journal*. 4, 261–69.

23. Epperson, D. C., 1964. A re-assessment of indices of parental influence in The Adolescent Society. *American Sociological Review*. 29, 93–96.

24. Epstein, C. F., 1970. *Women's place. Options and limits in professional careers*. Berkeley: University of California Press.

25. Felsenthal, H., 1970. Sex differences in teacher-pupil interaction in first grade reading instruction. Paper presented at the meeting of the American Educational Research Association.

26. Ferriss, A., 1970. *Indicators of change in the American family*. New York: Russell Sage Foundation.

27. Friedan, B., 1963. *The feminine mystique*. New York: Norton.

28. Garai, J. E., and A. Sheinfeld, 1968. "Sex differences in mental and behavioral traits." *Genetic Psychology Monographs*. 77, 169–299.

29. Goldberg, S., and M. Lewis, 1969. "Play behavior in the year old infant: early sex differences." *Child Development*. 40, 21–31.

30. Goslin, D., 1969. Introduction. Pp. 1–21 in *Handbook of socialization theory and research*. Chicago: Rand McNally.

31. Graham, P. A., 1970. "Women in Academe." *Science*. 169, 1284–90.

32. Gross, N., et al., 1958. *Explorations in role analysis*. New York: Wiley.

33. Harris Associates, 1972. *The 1972 Virginia Slims American women's opinion poll*. A survey of the attitudes of women on their roles in politics and the economy. Louis Harris and Associates.

34. Heise, D., 1973. *Personality: Biosocial Bases*. Chicago: Rand McNally.

35. Helson, R., 1972. "The changing image of the career woman." *Journal of Social Issues*. 28, 2, 33–44.

36. Hetherington, E. M., and J. L. Deur, 1971. "The effects of father absence on child development." *Young Children*. March, 233–48.

37. Hochschild, A. R., 1973. "A review of sex role research." *American Journal of Sociology*. 78 (4), 1011–29.

38. Hoffman, L. W., 1963. "Parental power relations and the division of household tasks." In Nye, F. I., and L. W. Hoffman (eds.), *The employed mother in America*. Chicago: Rand McNally.

39. ———, 1972. "Early childhood experiences and women's achievement motives." *Journal of Social Issues*. 28, 2, 129–55.

40. Horner, M. S., 1972. "Toward an understanding of achievement-related conflicts in women." *Journal of Social Issues*. 28, (2), 157–75.

41. Kagan, J., 1964. "The child's sex role classification of school objects." *Child Development*. 35, 1051–56.

42. Kagan, J., 1964. "Acquisition and significance of sex typing and sex role identity." Pp. 137–69 in Hoffman, M. L., and L. W. Hoffman (eds.), *Review of child research*. Volume one. New York: Russell Sage Foundation.

43. Kandel, D., and G. S. Lesser, 1969. "Parental and peer influences on educational plans of adolescents." *American Sociological Review*. 34, 212–23.

44. Kohlberg, L., and D. L. Ullian, 1974. "Stages in the development of psychosexual concepts and attitudes." Pp. 208–22 in Friedman, R. C. (ed.), *Sex differences in behavior*. New York: Wiley.

45. Kohn, M. L., 1959. "Social class and parental values." *American Journal of Sociology*. 64, 337–51.

46. Levitin, T., and J. Chananie, 1972. "Responses of female primary school teachers to sex-typed behaviors in male and female children." *Child Development*. 43, 1309–16.

47. Lewis, M., 1972. "Parents and children: sex-role development." *School Review* 80, 2, 229–40.

48. Maccoby, E. E., 1964. "Effects of the mass media." Pp. 323–49 in Hoffman, M. L., and L. W. Hoffman (eds.),

Review of child development research. Volume one. New York: Russell Sage Foundation.

49. Maccoby, E. E., and C. N. Jacklin, 1973. "Stress, activity and proximity seeking: sex differences in the year-old child." *Child Development*. 44, 34–42.

50. ———, 1974. "What we know and don't know about sex differences." *Psychology Today,* December, 109–12.

51. ———, 1974. *The psychology of sex differences*. Stanford: Stanford University Press.

52. McCord, J., W. McCord, and E. Thurber, 1962. "Some effects of paternal absence on male children." *Journal of Abnormal Social Psychology*. 64, 361–69.

53. Messick, S., 1972. "What kind of difference does sex make?" Pp. 2–8 in Anderson, S. (ed.)., *Sex differences and discrimination in education*. Worthington, Ohio: Charles A. Jones Publishing Company.

54. Meyer, W. J., and G. G. Thompson, 1956. "Sex differences in the distribution of teacher approval and disapproval among sixth grade children." *Journal of Educational Psychology*. 47, 385–96.

55. Mill, J. S., 1869. The subjection of women. Pp. 123–242 in Rossi, A. (ed.), Essays on sex equality. Chicago: University of Chicago Press, 1970.

56. Monahan, T. P., 1957. "Family status and the delinquent child: a reappraisal and some new findings." *Social Forces*. 35, 250–58.

57. Morrison, A., and D. McIntyre, 1969. *Teachers and teaching*. Baltimore: Penguin Books.

58. Moss, H. A., 1967. "Sex, age and state as determinants of mother-infant interaction." *Merrill-Palmer Quarterly*. 13, 19–36.

59. ———, 1974. "Early sex differences and mother-infant interaction." Pp. 149–63 in Friedman, R. C. (ed.), *Sex differences in behavior*. New York: Wiley.

60. Moyer, K. E., 1974. "Sex differences in aggression." Pp. 335–72 in Friedman, R. C. (ed.), *Sex differences in behavior*. New York: Wiley.

61. Musgrove, F., 1964. *Youth and the social order*. Bloomington: Indiana University Press.

62. National Education Association, 1973. *Education for Survival. Final report of the sex role stereotypes pro-*

ject. Washington, D.C.: National Education Association.

63. Oetzel, R. M., 1966. "Annotated bibliography and classified summary of research on sex differences." In Maccoby, E. E. (ed.), *The development of sex differences.* Stanford: Stanford University Press.

64. Parker, S., and R. J. Kleiner, 1966. "Characteristics of Negro mothers in singleheaded households." *Journal of Marriage and the Family.* 28, 507–13.

65. Saario, T. N., C. N. Jacklin, and C. K. Tittle, 1973. "Sex role stereotyping in the public schools." *Harvard Educational Review.* 43, 3, 386–416.

66. Sarason, S., 1973. "Jewishness, Blackishness and the nature-nurture controversy." *American Psychologist.* 28, 11, 962–71.

67. Sills, Y., 1972. "Beyond paranoia: toward the social science of Women's Lib." *The Columbia Forum.* Spring issue.

68. Sistrunk, F., and J. W. McDavid, 1971. "Sex variable in conforming behavior." *Journal of Personality and Social Psychology.* 17, 200–7.

69. Spaulding, R., 1963. *Achievement, creativity, and self-concept correlates of teacher-pupil transactions in elementary schools.* Cooperative Research Project No. 1352, U. S. Department of Health, Education and Welfare, Office of Education.

70. Stein, A. H., and M. M. Bailey, 1973. "The socialization of achievement orientation in females." *Psychological Bulletin.* 80 (5), 345–66.

71. Suniewick, N., 1971. "Beyond the findings." Pp. 11–26 in Astin, H. A. (ed.), *Women. A bibliography on their education and careers.* Washington, D.C.: Human Service Press.

72. Tidball, M. E., 1974. "The search for talented women." *Change.* May, 51–52, 64.

73. Tittle, C. K., 1973. "Women and educational testing." *Phi Delta Kappan,* LV (2), 118–19.

74. Weitzman, L., D. Eifler, E. Holcada, and C. Ross, 1972. "Sex-role socialization in picture books for pre-school children." *American Journal of Sociology.* 77, 1125–50.

75. Yankelovitch, D., 1974. *The new morality. A profile of American youth in the 70's.* New York: McGraw-Hill.

VI. SCIENCE AND THE WOMAN PROBLEM: HISTORICAL PERSPECTIVES

Elizabeth Fee

The Woman Problem

By the second half of the nineteenth century, industrial capitalism had reshaped the old sexual order in England. The changing nature of production had produced a new woman; in fact, *two* new women.

There was the working-class woman, pulled from the farm to the factory who lived in the growing industrial cities of the North of England. She was young, unmarried, and economically independent. She worked, not as women had traditionally, under the direct supervision of a parent or spouse, but rather for an impersonal factory owner who paid her a wage for her labor. The work she did, to be sure, was arduous, unpleasant, and very poorly paid. Then, too, her freedom from the constraints of family life was temporary—it lasted only for the short period between childhood and childbearing. Yet despite its burdens, wage labor provided the factory woman a modicum of emancipation from the traditional restraints imposed on her sex.

Contemporary observers remarked particularly on the degree to which economic independence had generated a new, more emancipated attitude toward male-female relations. Glimpses of the newer style can be found in the writings of reformers and critics alike, as in the censorious comments of Eliza Lynn Linton:

> Among the working-classes, the women at times rule the men with a heavy hand, and shrewishness fills the public-houses as much as slatternliness. I have myself known instances where the wife has had her

own industry separate from the husband's, and where he has given her board money for himself; and in all these cases I have known the wife both to grudge and filch from the food which she had to allow the husband, and hold herself worthy of pity and compassion in that she had to cook for him when she herself would have made up with bread and tea, and passionately abuse him for his sensuality, in that he demanded to be more richly nourished than herself (1).

The dimensions of the change should not be overstated; factory women continued to have fewer personal freedoms than factory men, and those were limited indeed. Yet such freedoms increasingly caught the eye of the *other* new woman who had emerged during the social and economic transformations of the early capitalist era.

At the same time that the changing order pushed the working-class woman into the labor market, the middle-class woman had been pulled firmly back into the home. A cult of domesticity demanded that the bourgeois female cultivate the gentle arts of femininity. The leading characteristics of femininity were abstinence— both abstinence from labor and abstinence from sexuality—and reproductivity, that is, the production of children. "The functions of the wife," went one formulation, "except among the poorest class, are or ought to be exclusively domestic." That meant she should "bear children, regulate the affairs of the household, and be an aid and companion to her husband (2)." Her social importance lay in her very idleness. Nonproductivity was a major indicator of class standing, a working wife a sign of social and economic disaster. Other activities also served as barometers of social status. A woman encoded the exact status and income level of her husband by the material of her dress. Calling-card distribution patterns between the ladies provided an accurate index to status rankings. Marriages cemented alliances between the old aristocracy and the newer wealth. A wife's task was to help her husband survive the psychological pressures he confronted every day in the marketplace and to preserve the home as a place of refuge from the frenzy of competitive striving outside.

Throughout the Victorian era, however, the increasing contrast between the lives of the women of different classes began to provoke a most unladylike envy on the part of the increasingly restless middle-class women of the "unfeminine" freedoms enjoyed by their working-class counterparts. This sense of dissatisfaction helped generate the Woman's Movement. Lydia Becker, one of the founders and shapers of that movement and editor of the *Women's Suffrage Journal* for twenty years, actually *defined* the movement's goal as achieving parity with working-class (and upper-class) women: "What I most desire," Becker confided, "is to see men and women of the *middle classes* stand on the same terms of equality as prevail in the working classes—and the highest aristocracy. A *great lady* or a *factory woman* are independent persons—personages—the women of the middle classes are *nobodies,* and if they ask for themselves they lose caste (3)!" In 1894, Sarah Amos declared feminism to be a movement from the bottom up: "You could not long have such a class as the free factory girls of England without the infection of freedom spreading upwards. It has already spread through the middle classes, and by many an agency is spreading through the professional classes, until it has at last touched 'Society'. It has come to stay (4)."

Amos was overoptimistic. There was to be no such easy emancipation of middle-class women from the chains of gentility. The new demands of women for political, economic, and social equality touched off an extraordinary debate—one that soon transcended the English scene and extended to Europe and the United

States—on the desirability of extending a variety of
proposed freedoms to women. Thus was born the
Woman Problem.

Science and the Woman Problem

The Woman Problem has been debated in a variety of
languages—theological, political, and scientific.

The most traditional idiom, of course, was theological. Those disposed to justify the subordinate condition
of women had recourse to a divine curse—the retribu-
tion visited upon the daughters of Eve, she who had
behaved so irresponsibly in the Garden. The divine will
was given hearty affirmation by the fathers of the early
church, and was reaffirmed again in the Epistles of St.
Paul. Nineteenth-century opponents of women drew on
a rich tradition. Those who struggled to improve
woman's lot could argue a millennial counterpoint: all
were equal in the sight of God, including women. Increasingly, though, the nineteenth-century feminists
began to abandon the theological terrain, and anti-
feminists struggled to keep the discussion within the
traditional framework. As one opponent baldly argued:
"There is no reason, except Divine law, why women
should be 'in subjection.' Let men once succeed in shak-
ing the faith of the women in Divine law . . . and they
will soon have fiends to deal with like the women of the
Commune (5)."

The dominant *political* language of the day was that
of Liberalism, and it provided a popular context for the
debate. As a language system it afforded feminists a decided advantage. Forged in the struggles of the middle
class against the aristocracy, it retained a strong critical
component. The logic of "all men are created equal"
could readily be extended to women. Feminist writers
like J. S. Mill and Mary Wollstonecraft argued that if

"natural man"—an admitted abstraction—possessed inalienable rights, perhaps natural man could stand for women as well. It is interesting to note that even a man like Herbert Spencer, who would later become such a strong critic of women's rights, favored the movement for equal freedoms and independence in his *Social Statics* (1850). He was rigorous and consistent enough in his logic to draw the inescapable implications from his individualist theory (6).

Most Liberal theorists, however, could ill afford the luxury of logical consistency; the impact on the social structure would have been as devastating as if the southern planters of the antebellum United States had admitted that the grand pronouncements of the Declaration of Independence should logically be applied to black people. A variety of reasons were advanced for exempting most of humanity from the status of "men." "Manhood" required a certain amount of property, which in turn produced qualities of independence and rationality; manhood also required the physical strength to protect that property. Women clearly lacked the entrance requirements, as did blacks, and working-class males. But these *ad hoc* adjustments destroyed the ideological purity of Liberal theory and laid it open to charges of special pleading. And there were always important Liberal writers, like the editors of the Westminster Review, who consistently supported legal rights for women.

There was a third context of debate on the Woman Problem, however: the language of science. Comte had argued that the scientific mode was both the latest and the most reliable form of knowledge, surpassing both the religious and the metaphysical (by which he meant theorizing that abstracted from social conditions, as in political philosophy). Whether or not many accepted or even studied Comte's philosophy, his categories accurately reflected the arenas of intellectual debate. The central epistemological struggles of the day centered on the rival claims of theology, political philosophy, and science to be the pre-eminent mode of thought and authority. The furor over Charles Darwin's *On the Origin of Species* was both symbolic of the struggle and its main event. By the second half of the nineteenth century, science was moving toward ascendancy. In the eighteenth century, science had had to respect theological boundaries concerning, for example, the age of the earth; a century later their positions were reversed and theology was having to adapt to the scientific world view. Scientists then attacked Liberalism as vague, groundless, a mere logical game that adhered to none of the proper canons of scientific proof and evidence. Science pronounced its methodology superior; in particular it provided an approach to the great social questions which was calm, unimpassioned, and objective.

What did "Science" have to say about the Woman Problem? That depended on who the scientists were. Some, like Marx, Engels, and other exponents of "scientific socialism" supported the claims of female equality. But the great bulk of Victorian scientists—overwhelmingly middle class and male—sought to use the calm, dispassionate truths of science to prove that the demands of feminist "agitators" were founded on unscientific claims about the capabilities of women. Scientists in areas as diverse as zoology, embryology, physiology, heredity, anthropology, and psychology had little difficulty in proving that the pattern of male-female relations that characterized the English middle classes was natural, inevitable, and progressive. The very existence of the genteel lady, moreover, proved the decided superiority of bourgeois culture over that of the working class.

The Evolutionary Era: 1860–90

Most of the diverse sociobiological sciences shared a common intellectual framework—the evolutionary orientation. While the notion that the history of humanity was a story of continual progressive development was an old one, particularly popular in the eighteenth century, evolutionary explanations gained increased status and popularity after the 1859 publication of Darwin's *On the Origin of Species*. Darwin's grounding of what had been a metaphysical or historical doctrine in the material process of natural selection was seized upon by all manner of scientific and social investigators. His relatively precise assumptions swiftly blurred and evolution became a concept that stood for the inevitability and preferability of any slow, progressive change from a simple to an ever more complex state.

The popularity of the concept of evolution reflected the accuracy with which it described and justified to the English middle class the position in which they found themselves. The latter half of the nineteenth century saw them at their economic and political peak of strength and security, both at home, vis à vis the working class, and abroad, vis à vis other capitalist nations. Victorian intellectuals absorbed and mirrored the self-confidence of their class. They and, increasingly, their counterparts in the United States, Germany, and France, confidently sat astride world civilization. From that vantage point, the assumptions of evolutionary theory seemed extremely plausible. Then, too, evolution prescribed the proper measures for dealing with those social problems that remained. They would and should be solved by future progress, and not by any sudden, unnatural alterations in the status quo. "We desire," wrote one evolutionist, "to advance the race along the lines of its development hitherto, sure that in evolution, not revolution, lies the safety of our country (7)."

This general mood of optimism—based both on observation and desire—colored the scientific efforts of the period, particularly those dealing with social questions. The usual analytical approach consisted of constructing evolutionary scales which began in "primitive" times and progressed slowly up to a state of "civilization."

One of the "social problems" which the scientists tackled vigorously was the newly raised Woman Problem; quite often their investigations explicitly sought to rebut feminist claims to equality of rights. Their general approach was to define the genteel lady—the angel of the home—as the acme of civilization, the product of a long evolutionary process. They were particularly concerned to show that the removal of women from the work force was one of the clearest signs of social progress; the working-class woman (and by implication her entire class) they defined as either an evolutionary anomaly or a clear throwback to barbarism. The scientists, we will see, were both describing and applauding a particular historical development, the exclusion of middle-class women from the marketplace.

The Biological Sciences

One of the central themes of the evolutionary literature was the increasing sexual division of labor. From a primitive similarity and equality, males and females rapidly differentiated as one went up the evolutionary scale. Males became more aggressive, more intelligent. Females devoted themselves increasingly to child rearing and let the males protect them. The end point of sexual differentiation was finally reached in the sexual relationships characteristic of civilization—that is to say, of the Victorian middle classes.

The seeds for this concept were laid by Darwin himself in his *The Descent of Man and Selection in Relation to Sex* (1871). The greater part of his two-volume study was devoted to a minutely detailed account and explanation of animal sexual differences.

In "the lower divisions" of the animal kingdom, Darwin observed, organisms reproduced asexually. As one moved "up" the ladder of complexity, sexual reproduction was slowly established. First sexual reproduction was accomplished by the conjugation of identical organisms. Then the gradual differentiation of each partner led to two separate and distinct sexes, which gradually became more and more specialized in form and function. When one reached the level of the insects, fishes, reptiles, birds, and mammals, differences between the sexes were marked.

What were the chief differences? "The males," Darwin suggested, "are almost always the wooers; and they alone are armed with special weapons for fighting with their rivals. They are generally stronger and larger than the females, and are endowed with the requisite qualities of courage and pugnacity (8)." In addition to the development of such weaponry as horns, tusks, spurs, and larger teeth and claws, the males developed various structures "for charming or securing the female," such as sweeter voices, or more brightly colored plumage. These male characteristics were selected and passed on in two ways. In fighting against each other for possession of the females, the best-armed males would win and thus pass on their characteristics to the next generation. The only way to account for the preservation of the ornamentation and melodic voices, however, was to assume the females (though Darwin found it "astonishing") were "endowed with sufficient taste to appreciate ornaments." As with the lower orders, so, Darwin tentatively suggested, with mankind. The processes of sexual differentiation and natural selection proceeded apace among "the half-human progenitors of man, and amongst savages." The males developed not only size and strength but "reason, invention, or imagination." "Thus man has ultimately become superior to woman." Darwin, in fact, thought it fortunate that the male improvements were passed on in some measure to both sexes, "otherwise it is probable that man would have become as superior in mental endowment to woman as the peacock is in ornamental plumage to the peahen (9)."

Darwin's sexual selection theory had its critics. Many objected that it gave undue importance to the female in the mating process, that it reduced aesthetic appreciation of beauty (a "higher" human development) to sexual attraction (a "lower," animal instinct). Alfred Russell Wallace, coauthor with Darwin of the theory of natural selection, later revised the explanation for male colors and ornaments in a more acceptable way. Either they were the direct outgrowth of superior male vitality and abundance of energy, or alternatively the females could be seen as having been specially adapted by dull and protective coloring to reduce their vulnerability to predators (10). But apart from such minor objections, the notion that evolution itself dictated an increasing sexual differentiation—that each sex perfected the characteristics most suitable to its role and function, that male traits so generated included superior courage, intelligence and resourcefulness, that female traits so generated included a passive maternalism—this complex of ideas was seized upon by Darwin's contemporaries. And few seized upon it more enthusiastically than those engaged in confronting and refuting the claims of the feminist movement.

One of the early uses of sexual evolutionary theory in this way appeared in the work of Herbert Spencer. By the time of his 1864 edition of *Social Statics,* Spencer had already begun to re-evaluate his early support of the feminist movement; by the 1870s he had come full circle. In his 1873 article, "Psychology of the Sexes," he advanced his new arguments in a particularly straightforward (yet circular) manner.

Spencer began with his conclusion: men and women were as unalike mentally as they were physically. For anyone to deny this self-evident and inevitable truth, he said, would be "to suppose that here alone in all Nature there is no adjustment of special powers to special functions." Woman's function was to raise children. Intellectual attributes were not necessary for that task, therefore they had not been developed over the course of evolution. Spencer went further: they should not *be* developed. To be sure, "under special discipline" the feminine intellect could equal or surpass the intellectual output of most men. But this would entail "decreased fulfillment of the maternal functions." "Only that mental energy," Spencer insisted, "is normally feminine which can coexist with the production and nursing of the due number of healthy children. Obviously a power of mind which, if general among the women of a society, would entail disappearance of the society, is a power not to be included in an estimate of the feminine nature as a social factor (11)."

In general, Spencer argued, women were a case of arrested evolutionary development. Their individual development, too, halted short of the level attained by the average male. This was explained functionally: women had to reserve some quantity of vital energy to meet the cost of reproduction. In addition to a generally smaller growth of the nervo-muscular system and thus a smaller capacity of the "mental manifestations," Spencer argued that woman as a type collectively fell short in "those two faculties, intellectual and emotional, which are the latest products of human evolution—the power of abstract reasoning and that most abstract of the emotions, the sentiment of justice . . ." (11:32). This accounted for women's inability to make judgments that transcended personal attachments, and raised obvious objections to extending certain privileges to women, such as the power to legislate or sit on juries.

Another disqualification centered on the desire of women to please men. This trait, too, was an evolutionary product. Primitive man, Spencer assumed, had been extremely strong, brutal and egoistic; the women were physically weak and so those "who succeed most in pleasing would be the most likely to survive and leave posterity." Women, Spencer thought, had habitually selected males who were the most powerful; if they had not, if they had chosen weak men, would not the race have deteriorated? Thus women's characteristic fascination with power; they had a greater respect for all "embodiments and symbols of authority, governmental and social." Women thus loved freedom less than men. The implications were obvious: granting them the vote could be disastrous to freedom.

Finally Spencer proposed that woman's "love of the helpless, which in her maternal capacity woman displays in a more special form than man, inevitably affects all her thoughts and sentiments." This trait Spencer thought conducive to social disaster—that is to say, to welfare legislation. Women would no doubt tend to aid the poor and the incompetent out of public funds, thus undermining their will to independence and individual responsibility.

Spencer refrained from direct attacks on the women's movement. He contented himself with stressing the need for scientific understanding of biological truths as an indispensable prerequisite to social action. But others were less hesitant.

In 1881, Frank Fernseed attacked the idea being promulgated by "certain political and social agitators" that the assignment of different duties and employments to men and to women respectively was a mark of the "subjection" or "subjugation" of the latter. Scientific research suggested that, when "calmly considered, [it] is merely a characteristic of all progressive development." In the lower sections of the animal kingdom, as among the mollusks, especially the cephalopods, and the insects, especially among moths and bees, the female is the larger, the stronger and the better armed. When one reaches the mammalia, the superiority of the male in bulk, weight, and strength is without exception. Other differences abound: males eat more. "I have known not a few men who have been quite uneasy concerning the small appetites of their wives or daughters, fearing it a sign of illness." Fernseed marched rigorously through pages of such distinctions, arriving finally at his conclusions:

> The superiority of the female sex is witnessed only in the inferior races of mankind and in the young children of the higher, and marks an inferior stage of evolution.
> The same is the case with the equality of the sexes, which occurs merely in imperfectly developed varieties and species, in young persons, in the decline of years, and in the lower classes of society.
> On the other hand, the pre-eminence of the male as compared with the female marks a higher stage of evolution. It occurs in the highest species and races, in the prime of life, and in the superior strata of society (12).

"These results," Fernseed remarked, "will not be welcome to the successors of John Stuart Mill. But when did a 'reformer' stoop to consider such trifles as biological facts (12:744)?"

Another assessment of the evolutionary status of women, by G. Ferrero ("The problem of woman, from a bio-sociological point of view"), stressed the need for an investigation of the Woman Problem based strictly on "Scientific Principles," the aim of which would be to determine "the natural conditions of woman's life." "Science," Ferrero argued, "should endeavor, by studying the peculiar characteristics of the individual, to find out what is, so to speak, the ideal role that the human being ought to play in the progress of civilisation"; once that great plan was rendered clear, one could define "complete obedience" to its rules as "the measure of the ascending march of civilisation."

The essential condition of women, he argued, was "the Law of *Non-Labor*." He explained: "As it is a natural law that the man must labor and struggle to live, so is it a natural law that the woman should neither labor nor struggle for her existence." This law followed naturally from the superior efficiency of a sexual division of labor; the female insect lays eggs, the male protects her while she does so, increasing the species' chance of survival. To be sure, among savages women build the huts, plow the fields, carry the burdens. But, Ferrero insisted, "this is merely a passing phase, a very dangerous aberration, produced by the excessive selfishness of man, which does not and cannot last long." Natives who act that way remain in the savage state; there is no progress.

Ferrero was also concerned to prove that the work of women in civilized nations was "unnatural" but admits the case difficult to prove: "it is so recent a phenomenon that the harmful results . . . are still difficult to

demonstrate." One point against the practice certainly is
that it "tends to lower the marketable value of male
labor; for, while woman is working in the factories,
there are everywhere, and especially in Europe, crowds
of men vainly seeking employment, to whom the cessation of work is an oft recurrent and terrible evil." He
also pointed to the physiological consequences, noting
"an increase of mortality among women and children in
countries where industrial life has pressed mothers into
its ranks." The life of a factory hand, he added, "is the
most dreadful imaginable, above all when she has
young children." Yet fortunately women are not, in
civilized nations, obliged to toil, "except in those countries where large manufacturing interests have produced
a transitory regression among the working classes." But
the lesson of evolution is clear; in time they too shall
become civilized, and then woman can retire to her natural place, the home, and become "the little queen of a
more or less extended empire, surrounded by homage,
veneration, and love (13)."

If on the one hand evolution dictated women should
not labor in the workplace, evolution appeared to insist
that she labor in the home. Walter Bagehot, writing in
1879 on "Biology and Women's Rights," made the customary disavowal of unconcern as to the ethical, sentimental, or political arguments used on either side of the
Woman Problem debate (though he certainly considered
it a serious question—"It is of no use laughing at this
agitation as the outcome of a mere 'crotchet.' In certain
states of the moral atmosphere crotchets spread just as
do epidemics . . ."). But the customary perusal of the
animal kingdom produced perfectly clear lessons. Males
were bold, pugnacious, adventurous, restless; females,
save in protecting their young, were mild, gentle, and
inoffensive. "Of this no more indisputable instance
could be found than the case of domestic cattle, the

cow—with the exception of certain 'strong-minded' individuals—being perfectly harmless, while the bull . . . is one of the most dangerous animals known, attacking and killing human beings, not for food, like the lion or the tiger, but out of pure 'superfluity of naughtiness' (14)."

After completing his review of the mammalian habits, Bagehot concluded that "the respective tasks of the two sexes are precisely such as we find in our own species: the male is the defender and provider, wherever such defense and provision are necessary; the female is the nurse. The man who brings home to his wife his weekly earnings, his professional fees, or his share of the profits of a business, merely repeats on a higher scale the action of the lion who carries a deer or an antelope to his den." Each sex fulfilled the task nature assigned it. "Anything like 'subjugation' is utterly out of the question." Thus the "attempt to alter the present relations of the sexes is not a rebellion against some arbitrary law instituted by a despot or a majority—not an attempt to break the yoke of a mere convention; it is a struggle against Nature; a war undertaken to reverse the very conditions under which not man alone, but all mammalian species have reached their present development."

Bagehot, too, knew that many women worked, but the example of the working class was a bad one: "The results of mothers withdrawn from domestic duties, and spending their days in industrial pursuits, have been sufficiently exemplified in our manufacturing towns." The children of the factory and workshop classes had suffered extraordinarily. It would be a disaster, too, to introduce "female labor into professional spheres." The lessons of biology were, Bagehot noted, the lessons of theology: the burden of woman was the sorrow of child-bearing, and attempts to escape it were anti-evolutionary. The woman's rights' movement, he insisted, "runs counter to Nature (14:213)."

Anthropology

Social and physical anthropologists reaffirmed the central evolutionary tenet that progressive differentiation of the sexes was the hallmark of progress. Social anthropologists found this message writ large in comparisons between "primitive" and civilized cultures; physical anthropologists sought to prove their case by painstaking examination of the shapes of male and female skulls.

The cultural anthropologists noted that among "primitive" peoples women differed little from men. They worked; and as a consequence they had well-developed muscular systems and broad bodies. Wasp waists, small feet and "delicacy of feature" apparently developed only with the rise of civilization. Savage women were also less modest; they had a greater affinity for sex. This was taken as clear evidence of "low status." The Victorians argued that only when women became less "like men," that is to say, when they stopped working and withdrew sexually, did one have a civilized society. The degree of civilization, that is, could be defined by the "status" of women. By such a standard the Western industrialized countries of course were far and away the most civilized.

The circularity of the reasoning is self-evident; had they chosen another criteria than "status," for example "power," or "economic productivity" or "freedom," their own culture would have appeared retrogressive. But one must remember that their argument followed hard upon their own observations and cultural presuppositions. Women, they knew from their own experience, did not like sex. Thus, almost by definition, the women of primitive society were being exploited; they were vulnerable to mass rape by any and all males. From their vantage point the development of the monogamous family put a check on man's sexual instinct. Women were protected by individual men and thus escaped sexual exploitation. Marital monogamy contrasted favorably with primitive promiscuity. Several of the most influential early English anthropologists directly linked the fortunes of women (and civilization) to the rise of strict monogamy. Most notable among these were John Lubbock (15), John McLennan (16), and Herbert Spencer. Given the assumptions of Victorian chivalry, that women were necessarily either the prey or protected possessions of men, the connection between women's elevation and sexual monogamy seemed self-evident.

Occasionally critics objected that even in the most advanced industrial nations women could be found engaged in those activities—sex and labor—which were supposed to have vanished with the rise of civilization. Prostitutes were busily serving the "brutal passions" of men, and women were trooping off to work in the factories and the mines. The anthropologists had a ready rebuttal: these were archaic survivals, remnants of a barbaric past; they were largely confined to the working class; they would gradually disappear with the further advance of civilized morality. As John Lubbock observed: "that which is with us the exception, is with them [savages] the rule; that which with us is condemned by the general verdict of society, and is confined to the uneducated and the vicious, is among savages passed over almost without condemnation, and treated as a matter of course (17) (18)."

A German and American variation on this predominantly English tradition saw not so much a progressive rise in women's status from primitive promiscuity to civilized monogamy, but rather the decline in women's social power from early matriarchal systems to more recent patriarchal social structures. This approach, associated with the work of J. J. Bachofen (19), Lewis Henry Morgan (20), and Friedrich Engels (21), argued that women had once exercised vast social and political power, when society had been organized along communal lines. This hypothesis did not require rejecting the central evolutionary paradigm. For, as Bachofen himself argued, though the matriarchate had been a period of peace, of harmony, of social order without coercion, it had been after all the childhood of the race. Children had to grow up. Patriarchy was less beatific, but it had been an advance and a necessary one; it represented emancipation from the mother (22). Female power, once again, had been turned into a sign of inferiority. As one analyst wrote, "the pre-eminence of the female sex over the male, occurring only in certain inferior species and races, and in children of the superior races, marks an inferior degree of evolution (23)."

It was, however, possible to read the evidence differently. Some feminists took comfort from the fact that women had once held a significant degree of social and political power. This held out the hope that they might again do so. The concept of the matriarchate was picked up by some American suffragists for its political implications, and Otis Tufton Mason wrote a feminist text, *Women's Share in Primitive Culture,* which emphasized the contributions of women to the invention of tools and methods for cooking, pottery, and agriculture. Engels, too, drew different conclusions from the researches of Morgan and Bachofen. Where others had considered the position of women to be in *inverse* relation to the amount of her productive labor, he argued that labor and status were *directly* related: "The lady of civilisation, surrounded by false homage and estranged from all real work, has an infinitely lower social position than the hard-working woman of barbarism . . ." (21: 43).

Physical anthropologists also hewed to the evolutionary line. Seeking to measure comparative intelligence, they busied themselves with measuring skulls, developing a "Science" that came to be known as craniology (24). Their researches affirmed that whereas the brains of primitive men and women were almost equal in size, male brains had developed considerably with civilization, while women's brains had grown only slowly. The sexual differentiation, moreover, was more obvious in upper-class brains than in those of the working class, more clear in white brains than in black brains; but in each case female brains were smaller than those of the male. According to the researches of LeBon, "the different social classes should be ranked by their cranial capacity as follows: literary and scientific men, middle-class men (*bourgeois*), nobles, servants, peasants (23:191)."

Increasingly the craniologists argued that women's brains were intermediate in size between those of the child and the man, resembling the child's more than the man's. This accorded nicely with Darwin's hypothesis that the female was the basic "race-type" of which the male was a higher development, or with Spencer's hypothesis that the female represented a case of arrested development.

The disadvantages and limitations of measuring intelligence by brain size were frequently recognized and as frequently overlooked. There was, after all, no other empirical method of rating intelligence. But it was certainly a convenient stick with which to beat the feminists, and was used over and over again throughout the period. As George J. Romanes wrote in 1887:

> We must look the fact in the face. How long it may take the woman of the future to recover the ground which has been lost in the psychological race by the woman of the past, it is impossible to say; but we may predict with confidence that, even under the most favourable conditions as to culture, and even supposing the mind of man to remain stationary . . . it must take many centuries for heredity to produce the missing five ounces of the female brain (25).

Physiology

One approach to female physiology suggested that the secret of sexual differentiation lay buried deep within animal and human chemistry. This hypothesis drew upon a distorted version of the principle of conservation of energy derived from physics. As we recall its formulation in Spencer's work, the theory suggested that each person had only a limited amount of energy at his or her disposal, energy which once expended in one direction was no longer available to be used in another. This accounted for woman's "arrested development." Women expended so much energy on reproduction that they had little left over to think with.

By 1889, Arthur Thompson and Patrick Geddes had elaborated a more "sophisticated" version of the metabolic argument which reinforced the message of the divergence of sexual roles. Males and females, they argued, were simply extensions of the characteristics of their primary sex cells, the egg and the sperm. Looking at the most obvious morphological properties of those cells, they noted that while the sperm cells were small, active, and energetic, the ovum was large and passive. They sought a metabolic explanation, but lacked the necessary experimental and theoretical tools. Hence they simply posited that these general characteristics were reflections of two opposite metabolic processes. Females were anabolic (they stored or built up energy). Males were katabolic (they broke down and used up energy). Thus they explained the process of fertilization by saying that "the essentially katabolic male cell, getting rid of all accessory nutritive material contained in the spermcap and the like, brings to the ovum a supply of characteristic katastates, which stimulate the latter to division (26)." Their schema encouraged a view of female capacities consistent with the energy scheme.

William I. Thomas, explicitly building on Thompson and Geddes' work, adopted the anabolic/katabolic framework, and used it to explain a wide variety of male/female differences. "A very noticeable expression of the anabolism of woman," went one of his formulations, "is her tendency to put on fat." More importantly her surplus energy is converted first into children and then into milk (while man's katabolism led to war and the chase). Intrauterine childbearing, moreover, expands the abdominal zone, and this forms "the physical basis of the altruistic sentiments." "The superior physiological irritability of woman, whether we call it sensibility, feeling, emotionality or affectability, is due to the fact of the larger development of her abdominal zone . . ." (27). Again the sexual division of labor was a natural phenomenon: "This allotment of tasks was not made by the tyranny of man, but exists almost uniformly in primitive communities because it utilizes most advantageously the energies of both sexes (27:62)."

Another approach to female physiology was the analysis of the female reproductive system. Before 1890, when there was no knowledge of the hormonal system, women's reproductive organs were thought to dominate their entire physical and psychic existence. Physiologists emphasized ovarian function, especially its periodicity, irregularity, and sensitivity, as being a key to the fragility of women. Far more sensitive and irritable than any other physiological system, the uterus could be upset by almost any external stimulus, including novel reading, excess study, the excitement of parties, late nights, and the tight lacing of corsets.

A review of the voluminous literature concerning women's gynecological problems and menstrual irregularities reveals several things: first, that women did suffer from a wide variety of gynecological disorders resulting from the birth of large numbers of children and inadequate or even dangerous obstetrical care. Second, many of the female disorders were relatively minor irregularities, molehills raised into mountains by the general anxiety surrounding the reproductive organs either on the part of the patient or the doctor. For example, perfectly healthy young women were advised to take to bed during their menstrual periods, so as to avoid "over-strain"; ladies' doctors took careful note of any menstrual irregularity as a sign of potential danger. Third, the symptoms which would now be diagnosed as "depression" were then likely to be attributed to some ovarian disfunction. And finally, more serious psychosexual disorders such as hysteria were also held to be caused by irritation or infection of the uterus.

The physiological link between psychic or behavioral disorders and the uterus was supplied by the concept of "reflex neurosis" propounded by the French physiologist Brown-Séquard in his *Physiology and Pathology of the Nervous Centres,* a series of lectures delivered in London in 1858. Mental disorders were caused by irritation in the various internal organs. Attempts to treat reflex neurosis generated a wave of surgical procedures against the cervix, clitoris, and ovaries by Sayre, Emmet, Baker-Brown, Tait, and other London surgeons. An eventual reaction set in when it became clear that most of the tissues and organs excised from women were perfectly healthy, and further that the operations rarely cured the original problem.

Surgery was one of the many attempts at finding a cure for women's illnesses. Metallotherapy, hypnotism, electrical treatments, bromides, rest, and seclusion were only a few of the other therapies popular during the nineteenth century. All were partially successful, none consistently so. Specialists in "mental science" recognized their lack of any systematic theoretical approach, but until the work of Janet, Charcot, and Freud gave new direction to the study and treatment of psychosomatic disorders, doctors could only experiment with the available techniques while blaming the female reproductive system and woman's constitutional weakness for her myriad discontents.

Those intent on political combat with the woman's rights movement seized on the medical testimony. One particular battleground focused on the early movement of women into institutions of higher learning in the seventies; American coeds especially were confronted with the argument that competition with men in the intellectual arena would damage their health. "Their nerve centers being in a state of greater instability, by reason of the development of their reproductive functions, they will be the more easily and the more seriously deranged," went one formulation. Dr. Edward Clarke of Harvard presented clinical histories of coed collapse in his *Sex in Education*. In one of his cases a woman student, with enormous diligence and effort, actually triumphed over all competitors, male and female. "But in the long run nature, which cannot be ignored or defied with impunity, asserts its power; excessive losses occur; health fails, she becomes the victim of aches and pains, is unable to go on with her work, and is compelled to seek medical advice." Rest helps, but it is too late. She cannot again regain "the vital energy which was recklessly sacrificed in the acquirement of learning; the special functions which have relation to her future offices as woman, and the full and perfect accomplishment of which is essential to sexual completeness, have been deranged at a critical time . . ." (28).

Henry Maudsley in England solemnly agreed. Dealing with the potential feminist objection that some women might in fact not care to be mothers, he replied: "they cannot choose but to be women; cannot rebel successfully against the tyranny of their organisation, the complete development and function whereof must take place after its kind. This is not the expression of prejudice nor of false sentiment; it is the plain statement of a physiological fact." The political conclusion seemed inescapable: "Inasmuch as the majority of women will continue to get married and to discharge the functions of mothers, the education of girls certainly ought not to be such as would in any way clash with their organization, injure their health, and unfit them for these functions. In this matter the small minority of women who have other aims and pant for other careers, cannot be accepted as the spokeswomen of their sex (29)."

Victorian scientists, then, argued for a strict division of labor at least for the middle classes, a division that sent the male out to work, and kept the woman at home raising children. This state of affairs they deemed the end product of millennia of development, and they condemned all attempts to alter it as unnatural and unscientific. To a large degree they simply applauded and legitimated the existing sexual patterns of their class and culture. For a generation their own observation and experience constantly provided reaffirmation for their scientific theorizing. As the turn of the century neared, however, both the terms of the Woman Problem, and the nature of scientific solutions, began to change.

Science and the Woman Problem in the Twentieth Century

While scientists propounded static theories about the unchanging nature of women, capitalists—the great modernizers—continued their relentless transformation of the economy, the polity, the society. The development, particularly in the United States, of the large corporation, the great banking houses, the big insurance companies and the giant federal bureaucracy wrought enormous changes in all areas of the culture; in particular it produced yet another transformation in the status of women.

The new economy and new technology demanded new kinds of workers to staff the corporate enterprises, mail-order houses, and advertising agencies. The economy needed secretaries, stenographers, cashiers, bank tellers, file clerks, telephone operators, office machine operators, payroll and timekeeping clerks, receptionists, and typists. In the 1880s women, many from the middle class, began to pour into this clerical work force. In the United States in 1880 the proportion of women in that category of work was 4 per cent; by 1890 women accounted for 21 per cent, and by 1920, for 50 per cent. The introduction of the typewriter on a large scale facilitated this movement of women into the work force (though invented in the 1870s, its use became widespread only in the nineties, as rapidly expanding business began to see the usefulness of mechanical writing machines). Typing was a "sex-neutral" occupation because it was brand new; women employed as typists did not take jobs away from men. In the United States, the number of women employed as stenographers and typists went from 2,000 in 1880, to 21,300 in 1890, to 86,400 in 1900, to 263,300 in 1910, to 564,700 in 1920, to 775,100, in 1930 (30) (31). In England, too, women moved rapidly into new occupations. They became commercial clerks in law offices and banks (they amounted to 0.3 per cent of that occupational category in 1861, 11.1 per cent in 1901, and 18.1 per cent in 1911). They became civil servants (4.1 per cent in 1861, 18.1 per cent in 1901, 21.0 per cent in 1911) and shopkeepers and assistants (18.6 per cent in 1861, 25.5 per cent in 1901, and 30.5 per cent in 1911) (32).

Clerical work attracted the unmarried women of middle-class background, who sought to support themselves until they married, and working-class women (particularly immigrant women in the United States), single or married, who worked to help support their families. Clerical and sales work paid better than most other positions open to women, and enjoyed a relatively high status (30:9–10).

The other major job category that expanded swiftly by the end of the century was teaching, and teaching rapidly became feminized. One consequence was that women began to enter institutions of higher education. In the United States, the number of women attending college rose from practically zero at the time of the Civil War to some 61,000—about 40 per cent of the total college enrollment—in 1900. About 43,000 of the "coeds" were in teacher training programs. In England, an 1895 study of female graduates of Cambridge found 680 out of 1486 engaged in teaching (33).

As women (predominantly middle class) began to enter the universities and the workplaces, they began to behave differently. For one thing, they married later and less often. In the United States only half the graduates of women's colleges married at all, and those who did had smaller families than other women of their so-

cial class. In England, also, only a small percentage of
the woman graduates of Cambridge married (33:956).
The Newer Woman also shed Victorian behavior patterns that kept her confined to the home for amuse-
ment, and took to bicycling, tennis, and other sports.
These transformations were widely noticed and remarked upon. Women, wrote one turn-of-the-century
observer, "are gradually invading all the fields in which
man had formerly no competition; and it is a new type
of woman who is competing—women who have accepted the necessity of single life and who throw into
their work all the energy which nature intended to meet
the drain of maternity (34)." The Newer Woman, in
turn, chafed against the innumerable restrictions that
inhibited her continued development. Her protests trig-
gered a new round of the Woman Problem. The roots
of this rebirth in the changing economic order were
widely perceived. Amy Bulley, a *Westminster Review*
contributor, argued in 1890 that:

> It is clear from what has been said that the po-
> litical activity now so strongly, and apparently so
> suddenly, displayed among women, is part of a far
> larger social movement. It is but one outcome of the
> ferment which, working in many directions, has urged
> women to demand and to receive a better and more
> thorough education, to adopt careers, literary, pro-
> fessional and commercial, and to take a part in public
> work of various kinds . . . With such an economic
> change, there naturally goes a corresponding change
> in sentiment, leading women to rebel against the ex-
> treme narrowing of their horizon which the domestic
> sphere has hitherto usually entailed.

The old order had been undermined with the movement
out of the home; consequently, and naturally, "social
customs and restrictions, which were harmless under
the old order of things, became inexpressibly galling

when women began to lead an active and independent life. Hence the cry for 'women's rights' . . ." (35).

What was the reaction to the political and social demands of the Newer Woman? There were two broad responses: vehemently unfavorable, and cautiously favorable.

Some critics saw the liberalization of the sexual codes heralding social disaster. Ferrero of Italy looked at the declining marriage rate of English college graduates and gloomily predicted the rise of a Third Sex: "English society will probably differentiate itself into two classes with different functions: one of women designed for the humble duty of preserving the species; the other of sexless creatures, intelligent, learned, industrious, but barren, living solely by the brain, with heart and senses petrified (Cited in 34:868)." There was anxiety about the fact that the sexes seemed to be getting confused; women seemed to be becoming more like men. Some men, too, seemed to be becoming more like women. The turn of the century was a period of intense concern over homosexuality; the immense public fascination with the trial of Oscar Wilde reflected that anxiety.

Others approved the movement of middle-class women to the workplace. Lester Ward, the eminent American sociologist, expressed the cautious rethinking going on in the United States. Responding in 1893 to Lambroso's plea that women be completely excluded from labor (the Italians were as far behind the times in social redefinitions as their economy was behind those of Western Europe and the United States), Ward admitted a natural compulsion to accept such a "chivalrous" position. But "such a crowd of practical objections at once arise," he added immediately, "that it becomes impossible to do so except in a very restricted sense." Pregnant women, Ward concurred, should be exempt from labor. But the notion that "one-half of the human race should be and remain, from the standpoint of economics, non-producers" seemed preposterous. For one thing, many modern women were unmarried, and they needed wages to support themselves (and, if widows, their children). For another, productive labor was a requisite for true health and happiness. Modern female work, after all, was not necessarily in factories; there was a "large and constantly increasing class of productive business which only involve manual exertion to a limited extent and largely consist in the exercise of various mental aptitudes." He cited teaching as an example. But in addition Ward advanced a new social argument: "Shall society lose the benefits which the peculiarities of the female mind enable women to confer in many of these employments, where men are less efficient?" The middle-class home need not suffer, either, for "the arduous part of home duty can be delegated by intelligent mothers to those who can do nothing higher." Here, indeed, was a whole new perspective: an expanding economy *needed* the labor of women, at least in certain areas (36). The World War gave enormous impetus to this rethinking of the proper sphere of women. Particularly in England, it was essential to have them in the workforce; 1914–18 witnessed a massive movement of women into the jobs vacated by men mobilized into the army (37, 38).

Scientists were divided; they responded to the economic and cultural sea changes either with an anxious rejection or a cautious affirmation of the new order. As a group they tended to be progressive, and willing to reassess the old Victorian evolutionary paradigm, which had so rigidly insisted on the inevitability and desirability of middle-class female idleness. Several factors pushed them in that direction.

Experience, after all, seemed to demonstrate that

many of their prior assumptions about the incapacities of women were simply incorrect. Female triumphs on the campuses compelled reassessment of women's supposed intellectual inferiority. As Helen Bradford Thompson observed in 1910, "even the time-honored belief that men are more capable of independent and creative work is beginning to give way in view of the successful competition of women in graduate work and in obtaining the doctorate (39)." Women's supposed inability to survive the hustle and bustle of the workplace similarly did not stand up. By 1908, the same William Thomas who had earlier written about women's anabolic inabilities was rhapsodizing instead about the talents of salesgirls: "Any one who will watch girls making change before the pneumatic tubes in the great department stores about Christmas time will experience the same wonder one feels on first seeing a professional gambler shuffling cards." Thomas also pointed out that "the fastest typewritist in the world is to-day a woman (40)." Scientists lived in the world and could not help but be affected by their daily encounters with the new woman.

Transformations in the scientific professions themselves fostered a hard re-examination of the old evolutionary assumptions. An increasing emphasis on experimentation, and a trend toward statistical precision, both fostered in the new university settings that mushroomed during and after the 1890s, led to a critical assault on the easy generalizations of the previous generation. Karl Pearson, professor of applied mathematics at University College, London, and noted for his statistical wizardry, was appalled at the shoddiness of the evolutionary investigations:

The fact is, that the word evolution has been so terribly abused, first by biologists, then by pseudoscientists, and lastly by the public, that it has become a cant term to cover any muddle-headed reasoning, which would utterly fail to justify itself had it condescended to apply the rule of three. A variety of ill-described and ill-appreciated factors of change have all been classed together and entitled the "theory" of evolution; they have been hailed as the expressions of great biological truths, and by taking a little of one factor and neglecting a great deal of another, any result might be deduced from the theory which pleased the taste of the user. Thus the door was opened for that loose, merely descriptive, and semi-metaphysical reasoning, which places a good deal of the biological writing of the past ten years on the footing of the medieval writers on physics (41).

When such sharp-eyed analysts confronted some of the specific studies dealing with sex differences they swiftly demolished them. Pearson, for example, entered the craniological debate over the relative size (and thus relative intelligence) of male and female brains. Between 1901 and 1906 Pearson and his students published several papers that by employing an exhaustive series of anatomical statistics effectively destroyed the presumed connection between brain size, cranial measurements, and intelligence (42). In 1909 Franklin P. Mall delivered the *coup de grâce* to craniology when he demonstrated that neither brain weight nor measures of convolutions afforded a reliable basis for distinguishing between brains according to either race or sex (43). W. I. Thomas wrote a caustic epitaph for the whole enterprise:

There is something very mournful in the labors of those scientists who have devoted their lives to the study of the brain weight of men, women and races on the assumption that there is a direct ratio between intelligence and the bulk of the brain. It would be about as valid to assume that a vessel of water and a vessel of lye of the same weight have the same potency, or that timepieces of the same weight are necessarily equally good timekeepers (40:146).

To some degree the willingness of the new breed of scientist to re-examine the old positions on women may have stemmed from the fact that a goodly number of them were women themselves. Some of the first products of the educational and vocational transformation then under way helped erode the scientific stumbling blocks that retarded further progress. Pearson's key assistants in his project were Alice Lee and Marie Lewenz. Other female scientists who have helped break the stranglehold of Victorian social prejudices on scientific studies included Helen Thompson and Georgene Seward in psychology, Karen Horney, Melanie Klein, and Mary Jane Sherfey in psychoanalysis, and Ruth Benedict and Margaret Mead in anthropology, to name only a few.

The evolutionary model, then, began to give way. But what replaced it? The general trend of twentieth-century science progressively narrowed the social and psychological areas that were determined by biological phenomena (Nature), and expanded the list of traits and characteristics that were produced by cultural conditioning (Nurture). No sharp cleft between the two modes of explanation can be pointed to; no neat and tidy transformation took place. The two categories blended one into the other. Increasingly, though, the "mix" that accounted for human activities was presumed to be more heavily composed of cultural and environmental factors. At the same time as the importance of Nature declined, the possibility of transforming particular behavior patterns (now assumed the product of the environment) by education or retraining increased. The ramifications of this trend for redefining woman's role were swiftly perceived. The course of such scientific rethinking may be illustrated by the transformations that took place within the field of psychology.

Psychology and the New Woman, 1890–1920

During the 1890s, craniological investigation began to give way before the battering of the new criticisms. Even before it succumbed, however, attention had begun to be redirected to a new area. J. McK. Cattell called for experimental psychologists to turn from skulls to traits, capacities, and abilities. Laboratory testing should concern itself with the measurement of what various human brains could *do,* rather than with what they *weighed* (44). A generation of American psychologists scuttled to their labs and began testing, though they were seldom guided by an informing theory. Broadly based on a nexus of ideas about sensory-motor physiology and associationism, the tests measured what one took in (sense perception tests), how one dealt with that information (memory and word association tests), and how one acted on and in the surrounding environment (motor skills tests). The experimenters usually used small population samples, and employed a bewildering variety of research methodologies. As a consequence, the results of experiments were often not comparable even when closely related tests were given in different laboratories. Yet the psychologists plunged ahead with enthusiasm, measuring, recording and tabulating results. One of the areas of concern was what, if any, difference existed between the sexes in any of the areas examined. Concern with the social and economic debates swirling about outside their labs was seldom absent.

In 1895, Professor G. T. W. Patrick of the University

of Iowa summed up the state of the science to date on
the subject of sex differences. He was particularly concerned to bring the results of the studies done on the
psychology of women to bear on "a popular movement,
whose end, apparently being very rapidly realized, is the
advancement of woman to a position of complete political, legal, educational, and social parity with man (45)."

Patrick had one foot firmly planted in the old Victorian order and he gave prominence to woman's
arrested development, her intuition, her charitable im-
pulses, and the like. But the new order clearly made its
way into his pages. Everywhere the scientific testing
seemed to show that while women were indeed inferior,
they were not all *that* inferior; that while women were
different, they were often different in complementary
and useful ways. In addition, the studies seldom produced a unanimous verdict.

Regarding the senses, "the popular opinion that
woman's sensibility is finer than man's does not seem to
be verified by experiment." Women seemed to have a
finer sense of taste, men to be superior in delicacy of
smell (though investigators differed on both points); on
sight and hearing, "no conclusive results have been obtained," although Patrick did call attention to the fact
that "piano tuners, and tea and wine tasters, are almost
always men (45:213)." Moving to motor skills, he
found that the evidence suggested a slight lead for the
males. Gilbert had studied motor ability in twelve hundred New Haven school children, seeking to determine
"the number of taps that could be made in five seconds
with the finger" (an interesting test in the dawning age
of the typewriter). Boys excelled, but not by much: the
average number of taps was 29.4 versus 26.9. This lag
in dexterity seemed borne out by the experience of "the
cigar and cigarette trades of English manufacturing centers [where] large numbers of women are employed,

but are set to the coarser and lower grades of work, men being required to make the finer grades of cigars and to fold the narrow margins of the cigarette papers." Reinforcement came too from the "laboratories in coeducational institutions [where instructors] with few exceptions pronounce the men to be far more skillful in the use of the microscope and all other delicate instruments and to require less direction in the prosecution of their work (45)."

Turning to mental processes, Patrick found that men had better judgment and analytical capacity while women had better memory. "If fifty men and fifty women be required to write as rapidly as possible one hundred words without time for thought, in the women's lists more than in the men's will be found words relating to the concrete rather than the abstract. . . ." Women apparently "lack logical feeling" so that "analysis is relatively distasteful to them, and they less readily comprehend the relation of the part to the whole." Woman's memory, however, was superior, and she was also more diligent: "experience in coeducational institutions shows that women are more faithful and punctilious than men, and at least equally apt."

Patrick drew the appropriate occupational moral. "Woman," he declared, "owing to her greater patience, her intuition, and her retentive memory, as well as her constant association with the young, is especially qualified for teaching and has equal or greater success in this work than man." He could not refrain, however, from pointing out that "all educational reforms, from the kindergarten to the university, have originated with [men]." Patrick also affirmed that "in many kinds of routine work, especially that requiring patience, women are superior, but they are less able to endure protracted overwork." Politically, Patrick sat squarely on the fence. Science, he said, provided "no want of lessons for political and social reformers, if they would learn them":

> From woman's rich endowment with all that is essentially human, the most devoted enthusiast for woman's rights and equality might gain new inspiration. From her retarded development the educational and political reformer might learn that woman's cause may suffer irretrievable damage if she is plunged too suddenly into duties demanding the same strain and nervous expenditure that is safely borne by man, and if it is attempted to correct in a century the evil of ages (45:224).

This approach characterized many of the investigations of the next several years. Women could do more than had been previously assumed, but there were still fixed limits. James Swinburne typically laid out the precise occupational boundaries dictated by psychological experimentation when he observed that "many women can do some sort of scientific work. They are more careful than men, and more accurate in taking readings. In this direction they make excellent assistants, and they could probably do the routine work of the assay, or city analyst's office, or of an observatory, better than most men." But though they were certainly qualified for this kind of boring work, when it comes to the scientific capacity itself, "we find women are simply nowhere." To be sure one was beginning to find, Swinburne admitted, that "ladies" names often appeared as author of papers," but they usually did so only in "subjects involving tedious but accurate readings of instruments," and they usually did their work either in conjunction with or under the supervision of men, though "much is made about it out of gallantry (46)."

In 1903, Helen Bradford Thompson published the most extensive study then available of sex differences in testing. Between 1898 and 1900 she ran a series of tests on fifty men and women students at the University of Chicago. Comparisons were made between the measured aptitudes of motor ability, skin and muscle senses, taste and smell, hearing, vision, affective processes, such intellectual faculties as memory, association, and ingenuity, and of their general knowledge in English, history, physics, mathematics, biology and science (47). Thompson found only the slightest differences between men and women—a certain feminine superiority in association and memory, a trifling masculine superiority in ingenuity. More importantly, what differences she did uncover she attributed to nonbiological causes:

> The point to be emphasized as the outcome of this study is that according to our present light, the psychological differences of sex seem to be largely due, not to difference of average capacity, nor to difference in type of mental activity, but to differences in the social influences brought to bear on the developing individual from infancy to adult years (48).

Growing boys were more active and directed toward learning of new movements, manipulating tools; the ideal of manliness encouraged individuality, independence in thought and action, and readiness to experiment. Little girls had "a less active existence" tending to develop instead certain sensory and perceptual processes. Girls, too, had to deal with the idea of femininity which bred a spirit of obedience, dependence, and deference. Social role largely determined psychological characteristics, Thompson argued, and thus declared that "the question of the future development of the intellectual life of women is one of social necessities and ideals, rather than of the inborn psychological characteristics of sex."

Thompson's work swiftly became the classic of the genre, and other researchers began to report similar conclusions. W. I. Thomas argued in 1908 that "the fact remains that there is no type of mental activity in which the average member of any race or either sex cannot become proficient with practice (49)." There were certainly observable differences in capacity; woman was, on the average, "the mental inferior of man" but "not on account of inherent psychological defects but through her seclusion and limited experience, just as the European peasant in his seclusion becomes dull in comparison with the scientist in his more varied world." It is easy to see from this remark that the shift to environmental explanations did not automatically lead to assumptions of equality; one could still point to the difficulties of women doing the same work as men. Thomas again: "The woman who undertakes to do man's work to-day undertakes to compete with professionals and has about the same relation to man that the amateur has to the professional in games."

Still, the new analysis clearly suggested that many of women's actual deficiencies could be remedied by education—at least up to a point. Edward Thorndike, the great educational psychologist, provides an example of the degree of adjustment which the psychological profession found comfortable. Thorndike, in a 1906 essay on sex in education, took issue with the notion that differences between men and women "found under present social and industrial conditions" were inherently characteristic of the sexes. To be sure they differed, "but again and again one finds evidence that the qualities in question are not so much born in women as taught to them by the conventions of our present mode of life." Thorndike himself had studied thousands of boys and girls and had found that "the differences in sheer intellectual capacity are too small to be of any great practical importance to educational theory or practice." Thorndike proceeded to draw some radical conclusions.

> . . . it has often been argued that because women do or because women should manage households and rear children, they cannot learn to be lawyers, editors or engineers. But the fact that some doctrinaire chooses or even that society as a whole chooses that women should be mothers and housekeepers rather than engineers does not prove that by nature they *cannot* be engineers. Experience indeed is rapidly making this *"We wish not, therefore women cannot"* fallacy ridiculous (50:214).

Yet Thorndike shrank from the full feminist import of his researches and observations, and dusted off the old notion, dating back at least to Havelock Ellis, that while the *average* woman was equal to the *average* man, there remained one crucial distinction. The male sex had a greater *variability* in intellectual capacity (measuring 5 to 10 per cent greater than females). That is to say, the highest and lowest ranks were filled by males. "Of the thousand most eminent intellects of history," Thorndike wrote, drawing on Cattell's study, "97 per cent are men, the variability which causes the monopoly of genius causing also the existence of twice as many male as female idiots!" Variability meant that "of the hundred most gifted individuals in this country not two would be women, and of the thousand most gifted not one in twenty." Thus, Thorndike opined, "though the women should capture the teaching profession, they would hardly fill its most eminent positions; women may and doubtless will be scientists and engineers, but the Joseph Henry, the Rowland and the Edison of the future will be men; even should all women vote they would play a small part in the Senate; a female clergy is a psychological possibility but a female pope is not."

Male variability put definite restraints on female education. When the more limited range of ability was coupled with "the probability and desirability of marriage and the training of children as an essential feature of woman's career," it became clear that

> The education of women for such professions as administration, statesmanship, philosophy or scientific research, where a few very gifted individuals are what society requires, is far less needed than education for such professions as nursing, teaching, medicine or architecture, where the average level is the essential. Elementary education is probably an even better investment for the community in the case of girls than in the case of boys; . . . On the other hand post graduate instruction, to which women are flocking in great numbers, is, at least in its higher reaches, a far more remunerative social investment in the case of men (50:213).

Thorndike then introduced a new (or old) element into the discussion: the differing "social instincts" of the sexes (as opposed to intellectual ability). He spoke of "man's instincts of independence, conflict, mastery and leadership" and woman's "instinct to nurse, protect and console."

In the end, however, Thorndike tentatively suggested that perhaps "the proper action of education may be to diminish rather than to intensify the sex differences of temperament," as well as those of intellect. Girls who "have been trained to a measure of scientific accuracy and logical consistency," he thought, would be better fitted for "the real world." Those reactionaries who opposed this notion were "perversely stupid" because they supposed "the one thing which almost surely will not be, namely that the present modes of social, industrial and domestic life will endure. The present training of young ladies would be an insanity if men selected their wives for fitness to be mothers or business partners, as in the future they very well may do." In a rapidly changing society, the safest course seemed to be a program of "rational experimentation" rather than "speculative and *a priori* reasoning."

It is clear that scientific reasoning on sex differences was changing, and when Helen Thompson surveyed the state of the field in 1910 she was pleased that it seemed to be "improving in tone." Certainly in the past there had probably been "no field aspiring to be scientific where flagrant personal bias, logic martyred in the cause of supporting a prejudice, unfounded assertions, and even sentimental rot and drivel" had run riot to such a degree. Recent discussion seemed to be shifting emphasis "from a biological to a sociological interpretation of the mental characteristics of sex (39:340, 342)."

Thompson also observed that the cumulative weight of the experimental studies was beginning to have its impact in the political sphere. "Those who feel opposed to allowing women full opportunity of mental development," she noted, "have accordingly shifted the stress of their argument from the personal to the social standpoint."

> The cry is no longer that woman will injure herself by the mental and physical overstrain involved in the higher intellectual training, but that she will injure society by reducing her own reproductive activity (later marriages, fewer marriages, fewer children, opposition between intellectual and sexual functions) and thus lessen the chances of the best element to perpetuate itself. The conclusion seems to be that it is the highest duty of woman to refrain voluntarily from developing her own intellectual capacities for fear of injuring society—a form of asceticism to which it is hard to subscribe (39:342).

On the whole Thompson proved a prescient forecaster. The tendency, already evident in the early years of the century, toward emphasizing environmental rather than biological factors increased markedly. This did not mean an automatic overthrow of all the old assumptions about the limited capacities of the female sex. It meant rather that the battleground shifted. Some social scientists would argue that female limitations were the product of cultural conditioning, and that education could overcome many of those liabilities that prevented her from competing successfully with men. Others would argue that while women possessed talents equal (or nearly equal) to those of men, "society" or "culture" demanded nevertheless that she confine her endeavors to childbearing and child rearing. Division of sexual labor was, though not biologically inevitable, environmentally more efficient. Sometimes the two approaches co-existed in the works of one analyst, as with the writings of Margaret Mead (51).

If those two refrains dominated the theoretical score of twentieth-century writings on the role of women, they were repeatedly joined by a biological *basso continuo* in the lower registers. The biological explanation made repeated returns from its exile in scientific Elba. The discovery of hormones seemed for a time to provide "scientific" basis for almost every distinction between the sexes. In the popular versions of the hormone theory which poured off the presses after the discovery of the sex hormones in the twenties, woman was held to be the prisoner of chemical substances afloat in her bloodstream that kept her in a permanent state of instability. "Estrin," went one version, "like an artist intent on beauty, gives women their characteristic shape, voices and their distinguishing hair distribution, as well as their specially feminine responses to stimuli and even much of their feminine psychology." Motherhood again loomed as woman's predestined role: "Hardly a cell in the woman's body is unaffected by estrin's physiological preparation for desired events. Repeated disappoint-

ments fail to discourage this hopeful monthly renova-
tion of the female generative organ (52)." Popularizations (and bastardizations) of Freudianism in the
postwar years also tended to argue biological handicaps
limited women's effectiveness. These arguments did not
posit an inferior intelligence for woman, but rather an
innately greater emotional instability.

The battle waxed and waned, repeatedly shifted
ground, definitively settled one question only to have it
reopened again a decade later. The entire debate can
easily appear utterly chaotic, a game without rules. Yet
although it is far too early to know with assurance, it
appears that to abandon the attempt to uncover clear
lines of direction and movement in scientific research
on women would be a mistake. For what appears to
be chaotic from the perspective of the internal, logical
development of scientific theory appears rather sensible
when viewed alongside of the changing social and economic definitions of the proper position of women.

If the story of the transformation of scientific attitudes toward females that occurred between 1860 and
1920 proves to be typical—a judgment that must await
a thoroughgoing investigation covering a much longer
historical period—then certain regularities might prove
discernible. It may be that scientific theories on the subject are rather closely related to the actual current status of women, that they tend to be concerned with either justifying or condemning that position, that they
tend to accept the given social and economic and class
framework as an unquestioned given background for
their research. It would follow that as the position of
women changes—a change most often generated by
transformations in the economy—scientists begin to re-
evaluate their previous conceptions in the light of new
social evidence. This latter process may be explained in

a variety of ways. Often it is generational. A new co-hort of scientists find that the older paradigm does not square with their perception of the world (as daily en-counters with salesgirls and college graduates made older theories, generated when women were confined to the home, seem ungenerous, out of date, old-fashioned, or just plain wrong). Or the social, and/or sexual, and/or class composition of the investigators might change.

If this process is in fact at work, if scientific theoriz-ing is—at least to some significant degree—keyed to the status of women determined in the social and economic arenas, then it becomes easier to account for some of the wild swings of scientific approaches to the Woman Problem. The status of women ebbs and flows remark-ably with changing economic conditions. During the First World War women trooped to work; after the war they were demobilized back to the home. The same proc-ess took place during and after the Second World War. It is interesting to note that in both cases scientists set to work during the war proving that what had previ-ously been considered to be biological incapacities fatal to women's work performance were insignificant. Thus a 1944 study of the impact of the menstrual cycle on workers found that "as far as scientific evidence goes, there is no reason why women's reproductive functions should interfere with the performance of social func-tions." Any actual impairment, the report argued, was the consequence of the "paralyzing" impact of "social stereotypes" on women workers; the handicap was "in-duced by culture, rather than biology." "Menstrual ab-senteeism, which today constitutes a war liability, is being successfully combatted by psychotherapy (53)."

After the war, however, the emphasis shifted to other arguments—hormonal and Freudian—which suggested that once again the woman's place was in the home. Perhaps the crucial question may prove to be why, how, and in what way, certain scientific theories are given public prominence. It may turn out in the end that neither biology nor culture are intrinsically apologies for the oppression of women, but that the unexamined political and cultural assumptions that are hidden in any given theory account for the nature of the conclusions. If so it will be the task of feminist scientists to unmask and uncover those assumptions, and relate them to the needs of an unequal social and sexual order to provide inequality with "scientific" underpinning.

References

1. Linton, Eliza Lynn, 1876. "Woman's Place in Nature and Society." *Belgravia* 29:362.
2. Aytoune, W. E., 1862. "The Rights of Women." *Blackwood's Magazine* 92:190.
3. Becker, Lydia, quoted in Helen Blackburn, 1902. *Women's Suffrage: A Record of the Women's Suffrage Movement in the British Isles with Biographical Sketches of Miss Becker*. London, p. 42.
4. Amos, Sarah, 1894. "The Evolution of the Daughters." *Contemporary Review* 65:515–20.
5. Cusack, M. F., 1874. *Fraser's Magazine* 89:208.
6. Spencer, Herbert, 1850. *Social Statics*. London, p. 173.
7. Sedgwick, Mary K., 1901. "Some Scientific Aspects of the Woman Suffrage Question." *Gunton's Magazine* 20:333.
8. Darwin, Charles, 1871. *The Descent of Man and Selection in Relation to Sex*. London.
9. Darwin, quoted in George L. Romanes, 1887. "Mental Differences between Men and Women." *Nineteenth Century* 21:661.
10. Wallace, A. R., 1878. *Tropical Nature and Other Essays*. London.
11. Spencer, Herbert, 1873. "Psychology of the Sexes." *Popular Science Monthly* 4:31–32.
12. Fernseed, Frank, 1881. "Sexual Distinctions and Resemblances." *Quarterly Journal of Science* 3:741.

13. Ferrero, G., 1893–4. "The Problem of Woman, from a Bio-Sociological Point of View." *The Monist* 4:271.

14. Bagehot, Walter, 1879. "Biology and Women's Rights." *Popular Science Monthly* 14:207.

15. Lubbock, John, 1870. *The Origin of Civilization and the Primitive Condition of Man*. London.

16. McLennan, John, 1865. *Primitive Marriage: An Inquiry into the Origin of the Form of Capture in Marriage Ceremonies*. Edinburgh.

17. Lubbock, John, 1869. *Prehistoric Times*. London, p. 561.

18. Fee, Elizabeth, 1973. "The Sexual Politics of Victorian Social Anthropology." *Feminist Studies* 2:23–40.

19. Bachofen, J. J., 1967. *Myth, Religion and Mother-Right*. Princeton.

20. Morgan, Lewis Henry, 1964. *Ancient Society*. Cambridge, Massachusetts.

21. Engels, Friedrich, 1970. *The Origin of the Family, Private Property and the State*. New York.

22. Fee, Elizabeth, 1973. "Mothers and Matriarchies in Nineteenth Century Anthropology." Unpublished manuscript.

23. Delauney, G., 1882. "Equality and Inequality in Sex." *Popular Science Monthly* 20:192.

24. Fee, Elizabeth, 1973. Science versus Feminism: Women and Their Skills. Unpublished paper.

25. Romanes, George J., 1887. "Mental Differences Between Men and Women." *Nineteenth Century* 21:666.

26. Thompson, Arthur, and Patrick Geddes, 1889. *The Evolution of Sex*. London.

27. Thomas, William I., 1897. A Difference in the Metabolism of the Sexes. *American Journal of Sociology* 3:60–6.

28. Clarke, Edward. *Sex in Education*, quoted in (29), p. 475.

29. Maudsley, Henry, 1874. "Sex in Mind and Education." *Fortnightly Review* 21:482.

30. Davies, Margery, 1974. "Woman's Place Is at the Typewriter: The Feminization of the Clerical Work Force." *Radical America* 8:1–10.

31. Braverman, Harry, 1974. "Labor and Monopoly Capital: The Degradation of Work in the Twentieth Century." *Monthly Review* 26 (3):48–59.

32. Holcombe, Lee, 1973. *Victorian Ladies at Work: Middle-Class Working Women in England and Wales, 1850–1914.* Connecticut, 203–11.

33. Gordon, Alice M., 1895. "The After-Careers of University-Educated Women." *The Nineteenth Century* 37:959.

34. Gwynn, Stephen, 1898. "Bachelor Women." *Contemporary Review* 73:866.

35. Bulley, A. Amy, 1890. "The Political Evolution of Women." *Westminster Review* 134:5.

36. Ward, Lester, 1893–4. "The Exemption of Women from Labor." *The Monist* 4:385–95.

37. Ministry of Reconstruction, 1919. *Report of the Women's Employment Committee.* London.

38. Home Office Publication, 1919. *Substitution of Women in Non-Munition Factories during the War.* London.

39. Thompson, Helen Bradford, 1910. "A Review of the Recent Literature on the Psychology of Sex." *Psychological Bulletin* 7:335–342.

40. Thomas, W. I., 1908. "The Mind of Woman." *American Magazine* 67:150.

41. Pearson, Karl, 1897. *The Chances of Death and Other Studies in Evolution.* London, p. 103.

42. Pearson, Karl, 1902. "On the Correlation of Intellectual Ability with the Size and Shape of the Head." *Proc. Roy. Soc.* 69:333–43; Pearson, 1906. "On the Relationship of Intelligence to Size and Shape of Head and to Other Physical and Mental Characters." *Biometrika* 5:105–46; Alice Lee, Marie Lewenz, and Karl Pearson, 1902. "On the Correlation of the Mental and Physical Characters in Man," Part II. *Roy. Soc. Proc.* 71:106–14.

43. Mall, F. P., 1909. "On Several Anatomical Characteristics of the Human Head said to Vary According to Race and Sex, with Especial Reference to the Weight of the Frontal Lobe." *Am. J. Anat.* 9:1.

44. Cattell, J. McK., 1890. "Mental Test and Measurements." *Mind* 15:373–80.

45. Patrick, G. T. W., 1895. "The Psychology of Woman." *Popular Science Monthly* 47:209.

46. Swinburne, James, 1902. "Feminine Mind Worship." *Westminster Review* 158:189.

47. Klein, Viola, 1971. *The Feminine Character: History of an Ideology*. Urbana, Illinois, 1946, 2nd ed. Chapter VI: "First Investigations in Experiment Psychology": Helen B. Thompson.

48. Thompson, Helen Bradford, 1903. *The Mental Traits of Sex*. Chicago.

49. Thomas, W. I., 1908. "The Mind of Woman." *American Magazine* 67:147.

50. Thorndike, Edward L., 1906. "Sex in Education." *The Bookman* 23:211–214.

51. Mead, Margaret, 1935. *Sex and Temperament in Three Primitive Societies*. New York; See Betty Friedan, 1963. *The Feminine Mystique*, New York, and (47).

52. Bell, W. Blair, 1916. *The Sex Complex: A Study of the Relationships of the Internal Secretions to the Female Characteristics and Functions in Health and Disease*. London.

53. Seward, Georgene, 1949. "Biological Differentiation of Male and Female." *Journal of Social Psychology* 19:164–5; Seward, 1944. "Psychological Effects of the Menstrual Cycle on Women Workers." *Psychological Bulletin*.

AFTERWORD

Michael S. Teitelbaum

A most influential method of the biological and social sciences is to measure differences between categories defined by theory as "relevant." Sex is surely one of the most common of these categories, along with age, race, and socioeconomic group. The study of sex difference in behavior has been an important component of disciplines as different as genetics, psychology, sociology, anthropology, and a variety of biological and medical subdisciplines. The fruits of these multitudes of studies have been summarized here, with the aim of reaching some tentative conclusions regarding the existence, the sources, and the significance of sex differences.

As noted in the introduction, the results of these reviews point to the utter inappropriateness of the narrow disciplinary approach to the study of sex differences. The social norms and the politics of the Victorian period continue to influence the structure of Western science, but such phenomena cannot justify a narrowly biological or narrowly socio-cultural interpretation of observed differences between the sexes. Sex is at once a biological and a socio-cultural phenomenon, and only a truly social-biological perspective is adequate to its study.

From this perspective, let us briefly review the current state of scientific knowledge on sex differences. Despite the speculations which continue to appear (especially in popularizations of science), there is no scientific foundation to the proposition that the conditions of mankind's evolution led to a genetically determined differentiation of the sexes along dimensions of intelligence, emotionality, and even "bonding" patterns. Physical, physiological, and psychological differences between the sexes do exist, however, and cannot be waved away by political ideology or simplistic socio-cultural determinism. The key question is not *whether* some such differences exist (no objective observer could doubt their existence), but rather how amenable they are to socio-cultural modification and how relevant residual differences are in a modern societal setting.

It is obvious that males and females differ in size, shape, genitalia, speed, endurance, and perhaps even metabolic rate. In addition, female metabolism is more obviously cyclical as a result of its characteristic hormonal cyclicity, in contrast to the more continuous hormone secretion pattern in the male. (There is some evidence of nonhormonal cyclicity in the male, but it is far less obvious than the hormonal cyclicity of the female.) There also is strong evidence of sex differences in maturational and medical patterns: females mature more rapidly than males, and have a higher probability of survival at all ages for which we have data (including gestation).* Fewer females than males are born in every society, but their lower mortality leads eventually to an equalization of numbers and eventually to a surplus of females as the cohort ages.

Some popularizers of the literature on sex differences have made much of the sexual division of labor in hunting and gathering societies, arguing that it is derivative from physical differences in strength and endurance, or from biologically determined psychological differences. However, the best anthropological evidence is that such

---

* In some data from developing countries, infant mortality or early adult mortality sometimes appear to be higher for females, but these exceptions (if real) are probably due respectively to differential malnutrition of infants by sex and to the high risks of maternal mortality in these areas.

differences are in practice insufficient to explain the sexual division of labor in hunting and gathering societies. A more plausible hypothesis is that the biological requirement of maternal nursing imposes a double role upon women—both subsistence and nursing. Women's subsistence activities must be compatible with nursing, which in hunting-gathering societies means that gathering activities are more suitable for them. Hence a fundamental division of labor in society may be a social adaptation to a simple biological fact.

All societies follow a pattern of socialization in which social norms are transmitted and inculcated into new members of the society. Since all societies are characterized by some sexual division of labor, and by the complex of norms associated with it, it follows that all societies socialize their children into socially defined sex roles. We now understand how powerful such role definitions can be in affecting abilities and behavior, although ambiguities abound primarily as a result of conceptual and measurement difficulties. Nonetheless in Western societies the evidence is relatively firm that males and females show small differences in certain psychological capacities, though not in "general" intelligence. For example, it appears from most studies that girls' verbal abilities mature earlier in infancy, and that from about age eleven female verbal superiority appears again and continues at least through secondary school. Tests of language ability, comprehension, creative writing, and even spelling show clear female superiority. Similarly, males generally excel at quantitative reasoning, visual-spatial orientation, and mechanical comprehension.

Male/female differences in personality are also found. For example, boys exhibit more physical aggression and, according to some writers, greater aggressiveness overall than do girls. This difference appears at an early age.

There are also marked sex differences in interests and values. In American society, men tend to be more interested in scientific, mechanical, political, computational, and physically strenuous activities. Women, on the other hand, tend to prefer literary, musical, artistic, social service, and sedentary activities.

These findings must be read with two important *caveats*. First, most of the evidence describes aggregate differences, with very extensive overlap between male and female distributions. Hence no justifiable conclusions about an individual's characteristics can be reached on the basis of these aggregate findings. Second, the results must be recognized to be time- and culture-bound, as the study groups are overwhelmingly drawn from Western populations of the past fifteen years or so.

The sources of these behavioral and psychological traits are not fully understood. Direct teaching of some behaviors is obviously important, as is imitative behavior on the part of the young infant. Yet however powerful the forces of parent-to-infant socialization may be, they are insufficient to account for the nature of some sex differences and for the early appearance of others. Hence contemporary psychologists increasingly view the mother-infant relationship as an interactive one, with the mother responding to the infant's "innate" characteristics as well as providing socialization stimuli. Most would therefore agree that some biological factors are important, but the biological mechanisms themselves are not understood. For example, hormonal differences do not appear to explain differences in aggression, and the lack of understanding of basic brain function makes impossible any biological explanation of differences in such attributes as verbal, visual-spatial, and quantitative abilities.

Thus observed sex differences in behavior represent a complex of biological and social forces—a tangled web which present-day science can untangle only at the margins. For sex differences, as for differences among races and other socially relevant social-biological categories, the most modern scientific perspectives show that biology is no more destiny than are acquired traits genetically inherited. The early biologistic determinism must give way to a more mature recognition of the evidence of forces other than biology. In the scientific study of sex differences, the deterministic and simplistic writings of the nineteenth-century biological theorists (or of their modern reincarnations) ultimately must yield to the probabilistic and interactionist view which best approximates the social-biological reality.

INDEX